Secrets of Healthy
Middle Eastern Cuisine

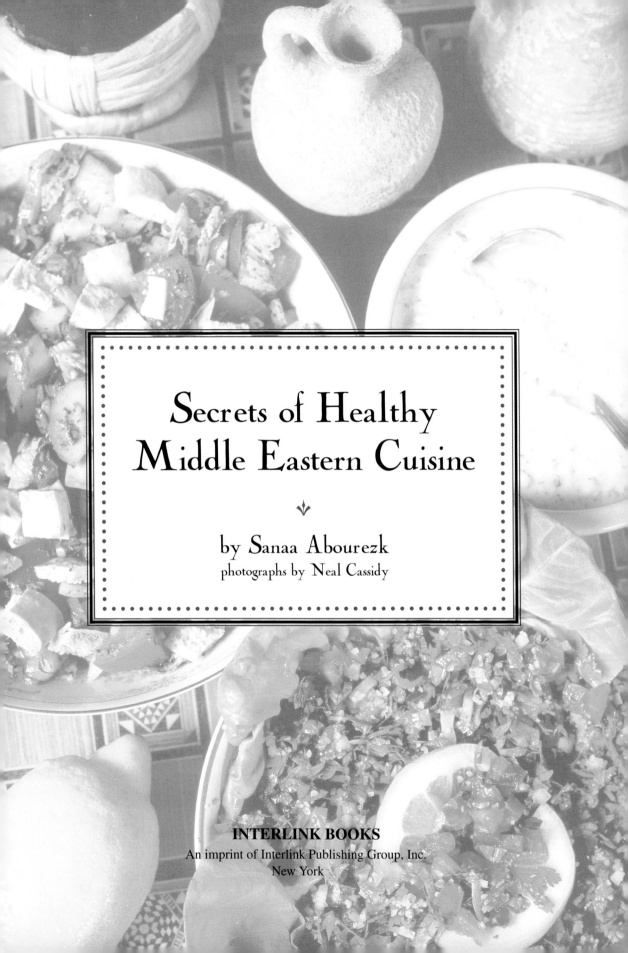

Secrets of Healthy Middle Eastern Cuisine

by Sanaa Abourezk

photographs by Neal Cassidy

INTERLINK BOOKS

An imprint of Interlink Publishing Group, Inc.
New York

First published in 2000 by

INTERLINK BOOKS

An imprint of Interlink Publishing Group, Inc.
99 Seventh Avenue · Brooklyn, New York 11215 and
46 Crosby Street · Northampton, Massachusetts 01060

Library of Congress Cataloging-in-Publication Data

Abourezk, Sanaa.
Secrets of healthy middle eastern cuisine / by Sanaa Abourezk.
p. cm.
ISBN 1-56656-310-0 (hardback)
1. Cookery, Middle Eastern. 2. Low-fat diet Recipes. 3. Low-cholesterol diet
Recipes 4. Low-calorie diet Recipes. I. Title.
TX725.M628A26 1999
641.5956—dc21   99–20256
                                                                          CIP

Printed and bound in Korea
10 9 8 7 6 5 4 3 2 1

Arabic quotations and calligraphy from Isa Khalil Sabbagh's *"As the Arabs Say..."*
are reprinted with the kind permission of the author.

To order or request our complete catalog,
please call us at **1-800-238-LINK** or write to:
Interlink Publishing
46 Crosby Street, Northampton, MA 01060
e-mail: interpg@aol.com • website: www.interlinkbooks.com

Contents

Dedication

This is the first cookbook I wrote, although it was published second. I dedicate it to my wonderful parents, Mahmoud and Shafiqa Dieb, who never gave up on me, and sacrificed everything they had to make certain that all of their children, especially their female children, had every opportunity to become educated. My years in school in the United States, my career as a nutritionist, my efforts at cookbook writing, all have come from them, and from nowhere else. Their love and support have meant more to me than they'll ever know. I know of no way to repay them for their sacrifices on my behalf, so I can only say, "Thank you, thank you, for what you've done for me." I hope they will understand how much I have appreciated them.

Acknowledgments

A few years ago, Albert Mokhiber, my husband Jim, and I were having lunch together in Washington D.C. The subject of cooking came up during the conversation, which led to a discussion of cooking from the Levant, that area of the Eastern Mediterranean that comprises Syria, Lebanon, Jordan, and Palestine. I mentioned that, as wonderful as our cuisine could be, it was loaded with fat. There is too much olive oil and purified butter used in the cooking. There is, I said, a much better way to cook our kind of food. I had, by then, been developing some low-fat recipes for my own use, substituting various spices that, while I used less olive oil, retained the great flavor of the original Levantine recipe.

Albert's eyes brightened. "Why don't you write a cookbook that features low-fat Syrian and Lebanese cooking?" he asked. "It would be a smash hit."

That was the germ that grew into this book. Over a two year period, I began experimenting with different ways to flavor Middle Eastern food while using ingredients with vastly fewer fat calories than the traditional. Even though our food is considered to be "health food" all over the United States, I knew that there was a better way. So after I moved to South Dakota, before my baby, Alya, was born, I began seriously to write this book. My wonderful neighbor there, Lori McGuire, who had five children of her own, along with my husband, was the official taster of all the recipes here. She waited, patiently, for each new recipe experiment to be completed, so she and her family could taste the results. That her husband is a medical doctor, and a gastroenterologist at that, was, I thought, the ultimate test. They ate up everything as soon as it was delivered to them, and each dish was pronounced excellent. I am grateful to Lori and her family for the help they provided.

Introduction

I marvel at how much Westerners spend on diet schemes, from books to complete diet programs that go beyond just recommending diet foods and concoctions for you to stay trim, but also offer them for sale. (And this, in the face of tragic starvation elsewhere!) We need not starve ourselves with liquid diets, with tiny portions that maintain, not a weight level, but a hunger level that eventually encourages us to gorge so we get even heavier than we were before we started our diet. My approach is that of most, if not all, nutritionists. If we are careful about the kinds of foods we eat, we can not only keep our weight under control, but we can also cut the risk of debilitating illnesses. As a nutritionist, I worry less about weight loss—the quantity of food we eat—than I do about its quality.

All of the scientific evidence tells us that diet influences the risk of falling victim to a number of major chronic diseases, such as arteriosclerotic cardiovascular disease, hypertension, and certain forms of cancer, in particular, cancer of the esophagus, the stomach, the colon, the breast and prostate. Proper diet combined with regular exercise alleviates the dangers of heart disease and non-insulin dependent diabetes. It also reverses the effects of cholesterol clogging your arteries, and prevents osteoporosis—the "widow's hump" that is the bane of older women.

Beyond these crippling and killing diseases, diet has an effect on the creation of tooth cavities and on chronic liver disease. Modifying your diet can reduce the risk of contracting something you do not want—which is one of the objectives of this book.

Another objective is to introduce lovers of good food to the cooking of the Levant: that is, of Lebanon, Jordan, Palestine, and Syria—my home country. Lying on the eastern shores of the Mediterranean, these countries share the Mediterranean love of toothsome breads and grains, fresh vegetables and fruits, fish from the sea, and olives from silvery hillside groves. Meat appears occasionally, and not necessarily as the centerpiece of the meal. Olive oil replaces butter. Since meat and butter are loaded with cholesterol, eating small amounts of them is more healthful than consuming them every day. The lack of them does not mean that Levantine food is short on flavor. On the contrary, eastern Mediterranean cooks understand the secrets of flavoring food with herbs and spices.

For those of you who are unable to travel to any part of the Levant, I want to describe what it's like to visit a spice market in Damascus, and introduce you to the folk or holistic medicine still in use in that part of the world. In Syria, the *attar* is the person who believes you can do wonders for your system with herbs and spices and who prescribes them as medicine. What is interesting is that the herbs sold as cures in Arab spice markets are used by drug manufacturers around the world as ingredients in their drugs.

A third objective of this book is to explain some nutritional principles, so when you read about carbohydrates, about cholesterol, about complete protein, you will know why we need them. When you know what is healthful, you will be able to make up recipes containing nutritious ingredients.

In the following pages, you will read more about the folk medicine of the Levant. You will also find dietary advice and healthful recipes, each complete with a nutrient analysis. Some of the recipes are my own creation, but most come from my mother and grandmother and from our family's neighbors in Syria and Lebanon. This book and these recipes will help you enjoy eastern Mediterranean cuisine in a most healthy way.

Chapter One
Basic Nutrition

Most of us would like to live forever, but that's a miracle not even nutritionists can perform. Try something more realistic, like staying healthy, and losing some weight so you will feel better. Better yet, try putting a hold on eating junk food, or butter and high-fat cheese and too much red meat. Try using olive oil for your cooking.

There's no argument among nutrition experts that what we eat and how much we eat has a major effect on our health. In fact, as basic as healthy food is to our existence, one would think that our schools would put greater emphasis on nutrition. As a nutritionist, I worked for a time in the Women, Infants and Children's (WIC) program in the South Dakota Department of Health. When I was seeing clients every day, I listened to people tell me over and over again that they cannot afford very much meat, yet they have no idea how to cook beans as a replacement for the protein provided by meat. I can hide neither my frustration nor my amazement at this dearth of nutritional knowledge. I really believe that good nutrition must be taught beginning in the first grade, perhaps even kindergarten.

Conventional wisdom has been that as junk food goes, so goes the taste. But, we now know how to make low-fat, low-calorie, healthy food extremely tasty, without the guilt and without the fat and calories people associate with good taste. It's pretty straightforward: If you cut down fat, if you use skim milk instead of whole milk, if you use non-fat cheese instead of high-fat cheese, if you use olive oil instead of butter, if you use non-fat frozen yogurt instead of ice cream, then, unless you are not of this planet, you will surely lose weight, and you will be doing your arteries a great favor in the process.

While most of the world's population is comprised of carnivores, we are now learning that we can stay healthier if we do not eat so much red meat. For example, I haven't totally stopped eating meat, but I make a point of not making a meal out of a single piece of meat. Instead, I use it more as a condiment to flavor vegetable and legume dishes than as a main course. The taste is there if you really crave it, but the great amounts of killer cholesterol are not. Cholesterol comes only from animal products, such as meat and dairy foods including butter, cheese and eggs. The trick is to eat the foods that have a minimal amount of fat, and, of course, to eat foods that are totally without cholesterol.

I know: You're worried about how to get enough protein if you cut down on red meat. But totally meatless, vegetarian societies, such as those on some Pacific islands, stay alive and healthy. Without knowing a thing about nutritional science, they eat a combination of legumes and complex carbohydrates, such as beans and rice, or beans and wheat, or beans and pasta. When such legumes and complex carbohydrates combine, they make a complete protein. In Egypt, for example, where few can afford to buy meat, fava beans and bread make up the protein-rich diet on which Egyptians have survived for centuries. The same is true in Latin America, where beans and rice have been a staple through the ages. Anthropologists have stumbled upon native tribes in the Amazon region of South America whose diet is mainly vegetable. The result is not starvation, but the complete absence of colon cancer, and very little heart disease. There's no question that our diet influences the kinds of diseases we inflict upon ourselves, especially the major killers in our society—cancer and heart disease.

THE AGRICULTURE DEPARTMENT'S FOOD PYRAMID

In 1992, the Unites States Department of Agriculture (USDA) finally released their "food pyramid," which established priorities for the food that people should eat. The Agriculture Department pyramid showed that the biggest part of our diet—the base of the pyramid—should consist of the carbohydrate group of foods, such as rice, wheat, bread, and pasta; the second step upward on the pyramid, it said, should consist of vegetables, then fruit; the third step is divided between dairy products and meat (as well as legumes for protein). At the apex are sugar and fat, which the Agriculture Department recommends should be eaten sparingly.

After spending millions of dollars designing the pyramid, (and after some heavy duty lobbying by the beef and dairy interests) the USDA finally released a basic food priority that has been widely known in nutrition circles for decades.

THE MEDITERRANEAN FOOD PYRAMID

A somewhat different food pyramid was developed and endorsed in 1984 by three groups—the Harvard School of Public Health, Oldways Preservation & Exchange Trust, and the European Regional Office of the World Health Organization. It is based on studies of peoples of the Mediterranean, who have low chronic disease rates and high life expectancies.

The Mediterranean pyramid does not suggest a specific amount of food to be eaten. Rather, it makes daily, weekly, and monthly dietary recommendations, then places more emphasis on certain kinds of foods. For example, it creates a separate category consisting of beans, legumes, and nuts, instead of lumping them in with meat, as the USDA pyramid does. Although the bottom segments of both the food pyramids are basically identical in emphasizing that you must eat bread, pasta, and other complex carbohydrates, the Mediterranean pyramid adds carbohydrates such as bulgur wheat, couscous (which is a form of pasta), and polenta, or corn meal.

The two pyramids begin to diverge at the next level. While both recommend that you eat servings of fruit and vegetables each day, the Mediterranean pyramid recommends that you also include beans, nuts, and other kinds of legumes. On the next level up, the two pyramids separate in a big way. The Mediterranean pyramid recommends a daily intake of olive oil—essentially suggesting that you should use olive oil as the only source of added fat. It also recommends eating cheese (the low-fat variety) and yogurt daily. Fish, poultry, eggs, and sweets are recommended a few times a week. The Mediterranean pyramid recommends eating small portions of red meat not more frequently than once a month.

Despite all the research that links red meat to heart disease, the USDA pyramid lumps meat with beans, giving the impression that all proteins are created equal. To appease the beef lobby, the USDA leads us to believe that eating a fast-food hamburger is as healthy as eating grilled fish or red beans and rice. Neither does the USDA pyramid distinguish among different kinds of fats; this leads people to assume that you can either use cholesterol-laden coconut oil or butter rather than the much healthier olive oil or canola oil. The Agriculture Department is the subject of heavy pressures from the beef and dairy industry, but we as individual citizens need not be. It is obvious that the Mediterranean pyramid is derived from what people in that part of the world actually eat, while the USDA pyramid, as imperfect as it is, and as much as its results have been heavily influenced by various industries, is more a set of recommendations than a study of what Americans really eat.

Understanding the kinds of food that go into your body may help you to understand what the food pyramids are all about. Try to imagine your body as a brand new automobile with all the oil and other lubricants it needs, except that it has no fuel on which to run. That is what your body is without carbohydrates. If you decide you want 1,500 calories each day, the food pyramids recommend a certain amount of carbohydrates and protein foods. If you tried to fulfill your 1,500 calories a day with protein, your kidneys would be overworked and ultimately damaged. Carbohydrates are the cheapest source of energy for your body and pocketbook, and should be used as body fuel, along with a certain amount of protein and a very small amount of fat, from olive oil.

Carbohydrates are essentially starches and table sugar. Grains, beans, potatoes, pastas, and some vegetables are called complex carbohydrates. But if you want to ingest simple carbohydrates, it's better to eat fruit than to eat table sugar. Fruit, as well as vegetables and legumes, will give you the fiber—another form of carbohydrate—you need to help cut down the risk of colon cancer, heart disease, and constipation.

Protein is the other key player in maintaining good health. Your nails, along with your muscles, body organs, skin, hormones, enzymes, and even your hair are all protein. But although our body is primarily protein, we only need 20% of our calories from protein. Animal products, such as meat, milk, and eggs, are sources. But there is a better source that will keep you much, much healthier—legumes mixed with grain. A mixture of legumes and grains, such as beans and rice, is a perfect replacement of meat as a source of protein. The two must be mixed, however. Eating legumes alone is not enough, and eating rice alone is not enough. Try hummus dip with pita bread or a falafel sandwich—these not only provide the body with protein, but also with a variety of vitamins and minerals and fiber, and very little of the artery-hardening fat and cholesterol.

Because fat gets most of the bad press in this country, we tend to forget that it does play a role in our body. Fat is an excellent source of energy. Each gram of fat yields nine calories, more than twice as much energy as a gram of protein or carbohydrate. It acts as an effective insulator, and maintains body heat in cold weather. As importantly, fat protects the brain and nerve cells. It carries fat-soluble vitamins, and since it is the last nutrient to leave the stomach, it delays the feeling of hunger. Even cholesterol is necessary for fat digestion, which in turn is important for the structure of the brain and nerve cells and for the manufacture of male sex hormones. But the sin most people commit is to eat too much fat; this is where we get into trouble.

The recommended daily allowance (RDA) of calories from fat is currently 30%. But recent research suggests that you can go as low as 10% and remain healthy. The Pritikin Center in Santa Monica, California uses no more than 3% of calories from fat in their diet. But Pritikin's program is under strict medical supervision and for limited periods of time; 3% is too low in a non-supervised situation. In medically unsupervised daily life, I think that dropping to as low as 15% of calories from fat will benefit anyone's health, without affecting the taste of their food.

There are three types of fat: saturated fat, polyunsaturated fat, and monounsaturated fat. The best way to symbolize these fats is to visualize a "fat octopus." The tentacles of the fat octopus continually reach out, trying to capture any floating hydrogen molecules. When the tentacles are all saturated with hydrogen, the result is saturated fat.

Saturated fats are solid at room temperature because they are saturated with hydrogen. Butter and margarine are the best examples. A good rule of thumb is that a fat that is solid at room temperature will break down into solid particles in your arteries, eventually hardening them.

If, however, only one of the fat octopus's tentacles has not grabbed some hydrogen, we get monounsaturated fat. Examples of monounsaturates are olive oil and canola oil. And if at least two of the fat octopus's tentacles are empty of hydrogen, the resulting fat is called polyunsaturated fat. Examples of polyunsaturates are corn oil, peanut oil, safflower oil, and many others.

All fats have all three kinds of fat within them, but in varying percentages. When researchers first discovered and publicized the various saturates and unsaturates, corn oil and other polyunsaturates took center stage because either manufacturers began hyping their products as oils that lowered cholesterol. This was a good news-bad news situation. In fact, polyunsaturates do lower cholesterol, but the problem is that they lower both the high-density lipoproteins (HDLs), the "good" cholesterol, and the low-density lipoproteins (LDLs), the "bad" cholesterol. Monounsaturates, such as olive oil and canola oil, lower only the bad cholesterol and do not affect the good cholesterol. Voila! If you want to consume oils that lower your bad cholesterol, use olive oil or canola oil. Of course, being from the Mediterranean, I was raised on olive oil, so my taste leans heavily in that direction. But canola oil also gives you the same benefit.

Cholesterol itself comes only from such animal sources as meat, eggs, milk, butter, and cheese. Our bodies make sufficient cholesterol for our needs, so we do not have to worry about getting it from food. On the contrary, a high cholesterol count spells trouble because the excess cholesterol is deposited in the arteries and eventually clogs them, causing heart disease or stroke. One of the components of cholesterol, the low-density lipoproteins (LDLs) are the culprits, so they are often called the "bad cholesterol," while high-density lipoproteins (HDLs) are called the "good cholesterol." In the manufacture of margarine, food producers sometimes add hydrogen to oils to make them more appealing as a spread. This extra hydrogen creates trans-fatty acids, which tend to increase the low-density lipoproteins, so such spreads, though based on oils, may be as harmful as animal fats.

Chapter Two
Some Tips for
Healthy Cooking

HERE ARE SOME TIPS FOR HEALTHY COOKING:

✦ Try to buy vegetables fresh on the day you plan to cook them, or at least do not keep them in the refrigerator over two days. Frozen vegetables are the next best thing if you cannot get fresh. Frozen items have little loss of vitamins, and, unlike canned vegetables, generally have no added salt.

✦ Parboil or steam vegetables before you sauté them. This reduces the amount of fat they absorb during cooking, and cuts the fat you need for cooking.

✦ If the recipe calls for frying vegetables, brush them with a minimum amount of olive oil or spray them with olive oil spray, and broil instead of frying.

✦ Trim off visible fat from meat before you cook it.

✦ If you are buying ground meat at the store, choose a bottom round steak or roast and ask the butcher to trim the fat and grind it for you. This eliminates a great deal of fat that butchers routinely add to ground meat.

✦ Try to use meat as a condiment rather than as a main course. To reduce the temptation to eat too much, divide any meat you buy into four-ounce portions, wrap and freeze them, and promise yourself that you will use only one portion to flavor a dish you're cooking.

✦ Remove skin from poultry before cooking. That's where all the fat is.

✦ When cooking meat, try broiling, baking, or poaching. These methods do not add fat.

✦ When making soup or stew, boil the meat a day ahead of time, refrigerate, then remove the fat from the surface of the broth before continuing with the recipe.

✦ Use herbs and spices rather than fat to flavor the recipe.

✦ When you find a high-fat recipe you like, do some experimenting with seasonings to get the flavor you like without the fat. Trust me, it can be done. For example, instead of using tahini, which has five grams of fat per serving, use my Cumin-Yogurt Sauce (page 78), which has no fat. The cumin replaces the flavor of the tahini. Similarly, many traditional recipes call for up to a cup of olive oil, but you can use just one tablespoon of olive oil along with garlic and spices such as oregano, basil, and thyme for delicious flavor without excess fat.

✦ If a recipe calls for cream, use canned, evaporated skim milk instead. You'll be pleasantly surprised at how thick this product is, despite its lack of fat.

✧ Using a slow-cooking crockpot for appropriate dishes will allow you to use less water and less fat. As a bonus, it doesn't require watching if you must be gone from home during the day.

✧ When sautéing food, use a heavy skillet and cook the food over low heat, periodically sprinkling with water to prevent sticking.

✧ Use either olive oil or canola oil in salads and in cooking.

✧ If a recipe calls for greasing a pan with butter, spray it with olive oil or canola oil spray instead.

READING LABELS

✧ Reading food labels will tell you a great many things, but primarily you should see which ingredient is used most in the product. The higher the ingredient is on the label, the greater the quantity. Most people should not ingest large quantities of salt, so make certain that salt is listed toward the bottom of the list of ingredients.

✧ The serving size suggested on the label is sometimes unrealistic. For example, if you read that a 20-ounce product has 80 calories per serving and the serving size is only half an ounce, that is a danger sign that should warn you against the product. If you buy it, you may find that the illusion of a low-calorie food will be shattered if you discover that eating the entire package is the only realistic way to feed yourself or your family.

✧ "Low-fat" or "fat-free" food does not necessarily mean low-calorie food. In order to compensate for the lack of "rich" taste in low-fat products, packers sometimes add lots of sugar, starches, or other high-calorie ingredients. Thus, some fat-free foods may nonetheless be high-calorie foods, and you will gain weight by eating them.

✧ If you are concerned about saturated fat, avoid items that use butter and lard and tropical oils such as coconut or palm oil.

Chapter Three
Herbs and Spices

ne of the great thrills I always experience when I return to Syria to visit my family is a walk through the Damascus market, *Souk Hamadieh.* It is one of the oldest markets in the world, with the black street stones still in place as they have been for centuries past.

Souk Hamadieh is perhaps the largest bazaar in the world. Think of it as a thousand boutiques along several streets, all covered with rusting corrugated metal designed to keep out the rain and the sun. The boutiques, however, bear no resemblance to what Americans call boutiques. They are small stalls brimming with whatever the merchants are selling at the moment. During its opening hours, *Souk Hamadieh* is a mass of humanity, with people of all ages working their way up and down the streets, eyeing both the merchandise and each other. There is virtually nothing that is not for sale in the *souk*, except perhaps, automobiles and large appliances. The selection runs from the cheap new to the expensive antique, from exquisite tablecloths and other goods made from damask, to inlaid jewelry boxes, backgammon tables, and musical instruments called *ouds* (Arabic lutes).

The merchants have perfected the art of hustling customers into their stalls. They all smile broadly, most of them singing out as people pass by, inviting them to buy their wares. Of course, no Arab merchant would dare operate his or her business without offering coffee or juice to customers— and that is true, not just in Syria, but throughout the Arab world.

On one of the side streets is a market within a market, called *Souk Al Attareen,* or the bazaar of spice salesmen. Along this street you can find not only every spice you've ever heard of, but many you haven't. You can also buy any kind of perfume you desire. If you take a bottle of expensive French perfume to an *attar*, he will compare it to the essences he has on his shelf, and sell you the one that matches what you've brought in. But essences are not their specialty. They also have herbal cures. Since *attars* learn their trade and inherit their businesses from their fathers and grandfathers, many of the essences and cures are from formulas handed down from generations past.

When I was in Syria not long ago, I interviewed an *attar*. He answered all my questions about herbs, essences, and cures, then asked if I was married. I told him that I was, although at that time I was still single. He asked if I had children and I told him I did not. He smiled and said, "Well, I know you university people don't believe in your ancestors' legacy but I am still going to give you this mixture. It is a spice of love. You boil it, have your husband drink it, and he will always see you as the most beautiful woman in the world and will never look at another woman." While I was sitting in his shop, women marched in buying cures for headaches, coughs, kidney and stomach pain, and one even asked for a cure for hemorrhoids. When the *attar* saw how surprised I was at the variety of medicines he was offering, he said "Some of them don't believe in doctors and are satisfied with what we offer here. Some even go to doctors, but take my medicine on the side just to make sure." Their philosophy was, according to him, that if one remedy did not work, *insha'allah* (God willing) the other one would.

The Crusaders, who invaded Syria and other Levatine countries in the Middle Ages, discovered the wealth of spices that had been imported by Arab traders from India and beyond. When the Crusaders returned home, they introduced spices to Europe. Soon Italian merchants were shipping them to Venice, which became, for a time, the center of the European spice trade. Since transporting them was expensive and difficult, spices were luxuries that only the nobility could afford to consume.

Today, spices are affordable and widely available. Here are some of those most frequently used on the tables of Damascus and other Levantine towns and villages. Most of them have medicinal as well as culinary value.

- **Allspice** comes from the purple-black berries of a tree that grows in South and Central America. Ground, it has a similar flavor to *bhar*, a blend of cloves, cinnamon and nutmeg.
- **Anise**, or *yansoon*, is used in cookies, bread and drinks, mainly tea. Medically, it is used to relieve stomachaches, to aid in digestion, and to increase the flow of milk for nursing mothers. It also relieves asthma.
- **Basil**, *reehan* or *habak*, is used either fresh or dried with tomato sauces, salad dressing, and *kibbeh* (ground up lamb, with bulgur wheat and spices), or as a tea. It is also used as a mild sedative, as it is believed to relieve stress.
- **Bay leaves**, or *ghar*. The bay tree was the symbol of victory in the Roman Empire. It was sometimes used to make a crown for the heads of heroes. In some cultures it was believed that if you put a few bay leaves inside an article of merchandise, it would be sold, or that if you wash with soap made from bay oil, you protect yourself from bad magic. Another old belief was that if a woman steamed in a bay leaf solution before sunrise, someone would propose marriage by the end of the following week.

  In the kitchen bay leaves are, of course, used extensively in soups and marinades, as well as for flavoring and tenderizing. Medically, bay relieves flatulence, and its oil is good for bruises, asthma, and toothaches.
- **Chamomile**, or *ba-bo-nej*, is primarily drunk as an herbal tea, as it is in the West. It is believed to lower body temperature. It is also a mild sedative, and it can ease menstrual pain. In Syria, chamomile

is used extensively to lighten blond hair and as a skin cleanser.

ᴠ **Caraway**, or *Ka-row-ya*, seeds, as in the West, are sprinkled in bread and cheeses. Its leaves are used in soups, tea, and salads. Caraway is said to help digestion, and to relieve headaches and colds. Women in Syria lighten age spots with it.

ᴠ **Cardamom**, or *hal*, flavors the famous Bedouin coffee, tea, and desserts. Some people apply it as a muscle relaxant.

ᴠ **Chervil**, or *sarfeel*, looks a great deal like parsley, but its flavor is not as heavy. It is sprinkled on salads, soups, and steamed vegetables.

ᴠ **Cloves**, or *qronfull*, are used in meat dishes and desserts. Cloves will soothe an aching tooth. They are also used to make tea.

ᴠ **Cinnamon**, or *qurrfay*, appears in meat dishes as well as desserts. Syrians believe it strengthens the heart and stomach, and relieves coughs. Applied externally, the oil eases aching joints.

ᴠ **Coriander**, sometimes called cilantro or Chinese Parsley, is *kuz-ba-rah* in Arabic. Coriander is the seed of cilantro. In the Levant, fresh coriander leaves are popular because of the desirable flavor and aroma. The ground seeds are mixed with other spices for sauces and meat dishes. Medically, coriander helps treat hardening of the arteries, and coriander tea relieves stomach gas. Some men drink coriander tea before ingesting alcohol, as it is commonly believed to increase their intake capacity.

ᴠ **Cumin**, or *kammoun,* is used with all bean dishes, both for the flavor and also to prevent gas.

ᴠ **Dill**, or *shubith*, is used in sauces, dips, pickles, and pastries. Lactating mothers use it to increase milk flow, and its oil, when diluted with water, is used to poultice hemorrhoids.

ᴠ **Fennel**, or *shamra*, is essentially like anise. It is eaten fresh in salads and fish dishes. The seeds flavor certain desserts. Medically, the leaves alleviate inflammation of eyelids. They are also a mild sedative, especially for children, and they are sometimes used to rid the body of worms. Cosmetically, the leaves are boiled and a pad is soaked in the liquid and used to soften the skin. People in Syria also say that when snakes come out of hibernation, they rub their eyes against the fennel plant to clear their vision.

ᴠ **Garlic**, or *thoum*, is famous in every part of the world. The ancient Egyptians drew sketches of garlic on the walls inside their pyramids. The Pharoahs offered it as a sacrifice to their gods and forbade people to chew it. The ancient Greeks gave garlic to the goddess Hykat to drive out evil spirits. Ancient Romans hung garlic around their children's necks to protect them from evil spirits. Modern mythology in America has it that garlic will keep away vampires.

The American comedian, Buddy Hackett, has said that if you eat garlic, the angel of death will never come to kiss you.

All that aside, there is no question that garlic is a healthy food. It counters high blood pressure, high blood sugar, and it cuts the accumulation of cholesterol in the arteries. Its antiseptic properties help relieve colds and infectious diseases. Garlic worked for me when I was stung by a bee. In Syria I was preparing to go to my cousin's wedding, in a strapless dress. After a bee stung my strapless back, my sister, a highly-trained endocrinologist, ran to get a clove of garlic, which she rubbed on my sting. I had no swelling from the bee sting, but unfortunatly no one came close enough to kiss me because of the overwhelming odor of garlic I emitted. (If you've eaten garlic and you are burning to be kissed, you can eradicate the garlic smell on your breath by eating raw parsley, raw cilantro, or licorice.)

Garlic is used in virtually every dish, but I especially like it cut up in vegetable salads. Of course, it should be used in tomato sauce for pasta or for the Levantine bean and rice dishes. Some people sauté pressed or chopped garlic in a frying pan just long enough to flavor the olive oil, and then they throw the clove away.

- Scented-Leaved **Geranium**, or *aatrah*, is an insect repellent. Its tea will relieve excess stomach gas. In cooking it is used to flavor sugar water.
- **Ginger**, or *zanjabeel*, prevents dental cavities and induces sweat. In Levantine cooking it appears in soups, meat dishes, and in desserts.
- **Lavender**, or *khuzamah*, is generally not used for cooking, but medically its oil helps when someone faints. It also relieves rheumatic pain when rubbed on the skin.
- **Lemon Balm**, or *mallisey trunjan*, is used in summer drinks and salads. Its tea calms the nerves, induces sleep, and sooths headaches.
- **Licorice**, or *a'aro-k al-sous*, is generally used to make a drink that is very popular during the fasting month of *Ramadan*, and in hot summer weather. Licorice drink salesmen are very famous in Syria as well as very colorful. They are noted for the castanets that they use to attract attention in order to sell their drinks on the street.
- **Marjoram**, or *mar-da-koush*, is used in stews, salads, and for pickling. It stimulates the appetite, strengthens the stomach and is good for headaches. Marjoram is also used to make soap, and when boiled, makes a tea, as do a number of leafy herbs.
- **Mint**, or *na'a-na'a,* is one of the best known Levantine herbs. It is used extensively in salads, with cheeses, in drinks, and in cheese pies.

It stimulates the appetite, strengthens the stomach, and when made into a tea, it eases menstrual pain.

↓ **Mustard**, or *khardel*, is used in salad dressings and sauces, with fish, and for pickling. When the seed is crushed, it adds its hot flavor to food. Syrians make it into a poultice for rheumatic joints, and into a soothing footbath.

↓ **Nigella**, or *ha-bet al-barakeh*, is a small black seed whose strong, nutty flavor is excellent when mixed in with homemade cheese (or factory-made cheese, for that matter). It alleviates flatulence, resolves fever, and increases milk flow in lactating mothers. It is also said to be good for asthma, and the smoke from burning nigella seeds repels insects. (Of course, any kind of smoke repels insects.) The Prophet is rumored to have said that, "Make yours the seeds of *habet al barakeh*, for it is a cure for all diseases except swelling (cancer) and that is a fatal disease." If nigella seeds are not available, you may substitute poppy seeds.

↓ **Nutmeg**, or *jozet al-teeb*, flavors both meat dishes and desserts. Some people in Syria believe that nutmeg clears age spots and freckles. But if this were true, nutmeg sellers would make a fortune.

↓ **Onion**, or *bussel*, was worshiped by the ancient Egyptians, who believed that the onion helped the dead to breathe again after re-incarnation, so they placed it in the pyramids alongside their dead pharaohs. They also fed it to their workers during the construction of the pyramids because they believed it gave them the strength they needed for their labor. I sauté onions and use them in virtually everything I cook. The wonderful flavor onions give to most foods is unbeatable. My grandmother credited her longevity to her lifelong intake of onions. Who would question a woman who lived until she was 114?

↓ **Parsley**, or *bakdounes,* is used fresh in salads, sauces, and soups. Medically, it is used in the Levant for flatulence, stomachaches and as a diuretic. Its leaves soothe infected eyes and insect bites, and removes garlic odor from one's breath.

↓ **Black pepper**, or *filfill,* is a favorite seasoning in the Levant, as it is the world over.

↓ **Rosemary**, or *hasa al-bann*, fresh or dried, appears in meat dishes, fish marinades, and salads. It acts as an expectorant when drunk as a tea.

↓ **Saffron**, or *za'afran,* probably the world's most costly spice, colors food yellow. It is used mostly in rice dishes and soups.

↓ **Safflower**, or *osfer,* is put into rice, stuffings and in soups, giving them a distinctive taste and an orange color. Medically, it relieves constipation and coughs.

- **Sumac**, or *sumaq*, is made from the ground-up berries of the Mediterranean sumac. The berries are burgandy-colored and have a sour, lemony taste. It is used in salads and with chicken dishes. In Iran it is sprinkled on fried eggs. Levantines believe it stops diarrhea and relieves hemorrhoids.
- **Tarragon**, or *tarkhoun*, is used fresh with cheese, salads, pickles, and in fish and yogurt dishes.
- **Thyme**, or *za'atar barri*, (wild thyme) is used in salads, with cheese, in marinades, and is one of the ingredients of *za'atar*, the famous Levantine herb mix.
- **Turmeric**, or *kurkoum*, colors food yellow. It has a strong, hot flavor. It is used primarily with rice and meat. It is also used as a diuretic.
- **Watercress**, or *jarjeer*, is mainly a salad ingredient. When dressed with olive oil and lemon juice and a bit of salt it makes one of the best salads you'll ever taste. Village women believe it prevents hair loss, and that it clears up acne in teenagers.

ZA'ATAR

I cup sumac
I cup thyme
I cup ground chickpeas
½ cup sesame seeds
¼ cup rosemary
salt to taste

1. Mix spices.

2. Spread mixture on a tray and roast it in a 350° oven for about ten minutes.

3. If you wish, add olive oil to make the *za'atar* into a paste for spreading on the dough described in the next chapter.

Chapter Four
Appetizers
(Mazza)

The food in the Levant—a region that encompasses Lebanon, Syria, Jordan, and Palestine—is the result of a great variety of influences, from the Crusaders, who flowed, uninvited, in and out of the region during the Middle Ages, to the Ottoman Turks, who occupied parts of the Middle East for four hundred years. The Levant also served as the historical crossroads of the spice trade between Europe and India, and this, too, profoundly affected its culinary traditions. The great variety of Levantine food is best illustrated in the wonderfully broad selection of appetizers, or *mazza*.

If you've ever ordered appetizers in a Lebanese restaurant, you will begin to understand the meaning of the phrase, "overdoing it." In Lebanon and Syria it is not at all unusual for the waiter to serve as many as thirty or forty different varieties of *mazza*. Appetizers such as hummus, (pureed chickpeas mixed with tahini sauce), falafel (ground chickpeas and spices, deep fried and served in a sandwich with tahini sauce), and tabbouleh (parsley, tomato and onion salad, dressed with olive oil and lemon juice), are just some of the dishes that have become accepted fare in the West. Interestingly, they are usually featured in health food stores, supermarkets and restaurants.

In a great many restaurants in the Levant, *mazza* is not a specific menu item. But if you order a round of drinks, and a main course of, say, grilled chicken or grilled lamb kebab or any of a wide selection of fish, the *mazza* appears automatically, very much like a roll and butter are served with a meal in the United States. There's also the danger of too much *mazza*. For every American I know who fills up with bread and butter before the main part of the meal arrives, I know ten (Arabs or Americans—it makes little difference) who gorge themselves on the *mazza*, so they are forced to abandon the main course when it comes.

A few years ago my husband, accompanied by his Syrian cousins, Ghassan and Hind, were on their way to visit my parents in Safsafi, the small village just south of Tartous, Syria, where I grew up. They stopped at an outdoor restaurant, Ain Mraizi, nestled on the banks of Syria's Mraizi River. The restaurant is famous for catching the fish that live in the river running beneath the restaurant, and cooking it on the spot. So, naturally, they ordered fresh fish for a main course then proceeded to eat their fill of *mazza*. They waited for the fish course, but after about two hours it had not yet been served. Because they were full from the *mazza*, and because so much time had passed, they decided to cancel the fish and leave. When Ghassan informed the waiter, he responded, "No problem, we haven't been able to catch the fish anyway."

On another occasion, a cousin of my father's visited us in Damascus, so my father took us all out for dinner. After he ordered a main course of grilled chicken, the waiter brought out forty or so *mazza* dishes. Our table was on the terrace, the weather was perfect, and my father was immensely enjoying the evening, so he kept asking the waiter to delay the main course. Finally, after two hours of *mazza* munching, he signaled the waiter to start the chicken, which, of course, took another thirty minutes, during which time we continued eating appetizers. We were completely stuffed, but somehow we managed to eat two of the three chickens that had been ordered. Ultimately, we all signaled that one more bite would kill us, so the waiter came to clear the table.

Now, for someone to fill a doggie bag with leftovers is considered a grave social error in Syria. So, our cousin—noted for being tightfisted— asked if my father would have to pay for the uneaten chicken. When my father said that indeed we would, our cousin grabbed the chicken from the waiter and, although he was completely stuffed, finished it off.

Enough, however, of *mazza* stories. It's time to lay out the recipes. I have collected here some of the favorites. Salads are also considered part of the *mazza*.

> Legend has it that a king once asked a
> wise man to plant something that
> would feed the nation for a year, so the
> wise man planted wheat. The king then
> asked him to plant something to feed
> the nation for ten years and the wise
> man planted a fruit tree. When the
> king asked him to plant something that
> would feed the nation for a generation,
> the wise man planted an olive tree.

BREAD
(KHUBUZ)

1 tbl yeast
1 tbl sugar
2½-3 cups warm water
5 cups all-purpose flour
1 cup whole wheat flour

Nutrient value per serving
(one loaf):

Calories	275
Fat	1 gram
Cholesterol	0
Fiber	3.7 grams
Sodium	4 milligrams

1. Dissolve the yeast and the sugar in ½ cup warm water. Let stand 2-5 minutes. Place both flours in a large bowl, and combine with some of the water and dissolved yeast. Begin mixing and kneading, adding water sparingly until a smooth dough results and the sides of the bowl are clean.

2. Cover with a towel and allow the dough to rise in a warm place until it doubles in size. Cut orange-size balls from the edge of the dough and form them into smooth balls. Cover and let them rise for 30 minutes. Roll into ¼-inch-thick flat loaves and allow them to rise again for 45 minutes.

3. Place the loaves in a 550° oven on a baking stone on the middle shelf. A baking stone, sometimes called a "pizza stone," is a flat clay rectangle, or circle, that can be found in kitchen specialty stores. If you do not have such a stone, reduce the oven temperature to 450°.

4. As soon as the loaves puff up, remove them from the oven and allow them to cool. The loaves can be frozen and heated later if you wish. They are just as delicious after being re-heated as they are fresh from the oven.

Yields 10 loaves

ZA'ATAR FLAT PIE
(MANA'OUSHEH)

Za'atar (recipe on page 19) is a Levantine spice mixture of thyme, ground-toasted chickpeas, sumac, sage, and oregano. It can be purchased in any Middle Eastern grocery store and some health food stores.

2 tbs *za'atar*
¼ cup chopped ripe tomato
¼ cup chopped onion
1 tsp olive oil
2 tbs lemon juice
1 loaf unbaked bread

Nutrient value per serving

(one *mana'ousheh*)

Calories	360
Fat	6 grams
Cholesterol	0
Fiber	5 grams
Sodium	110 milligrams

1. Punch out one unbaked loaf of bread dough (see page 24) and spread the *za'atar* on top as follows:

2. Mix the *za'atar*, tomato, and the chopped onion with oil and lemon juice. Roll the dough into circular loaves ¼-inch thick.

3. Pour the *za'atar* mixture on the dough and smooth it evenly over the surface, pressing it gently with a fork. Place the loaf on a cookie sheet and bake at 550° for 10 minutes, or until the edge of the loaf is golden.

Note: You can make smaller loaves. They make wonderful appetizers instead of, say, bread sticks or crostini.

شدِّ خُبزتَك واطلقْ عَبَستَك

"Take back your bread but release your frown."

25

FILLED PIES
(FATAYER)

Fatayer is a common appetizer made especially for parties. *Fatayer* are basically small bread-dough pies filled with meat, spinach, cheese, tomato, or onion, the name varying with the filling. Like bread, *fatayer* can be prepared and frozen in advance, then heated whenever needed.

BASIC PIE DOUGH

1 tbl yeast
1 tsp sugar
3 cups lukewarm water
6 cups all-purpose flour
2 cups whole wheat flour

Nutrient value per one ball:

Calories	81
Fat	0
Cholesterol	0 milligrams
Fiber	1.3 grams
Sodium	10 milligrams

1. Dissolve the yeast and sugar in ½ cup warm water, and leave it for 3 minutes.

2. In a large bowl, mix both flours and the yeast mixture. Gradually, add the rest of the water, mixing and kneading until the dough is smooth. Cover, and put it in a warm place for 2 hours, or until the dough doubles in size.

3. Cut the dough into 40 or so balls, 2 to 2½ inches in diameter. Form the balls by continually stretching and tucking the dough from top to bottom to make them round and smooth. Cover them, and let them rest for one hour. The dough is now ready to be used with various fillings.

Each ball makes one pie

WEDDING DOUGH

Because divorce is not only rare in Syria, but also devastating for the woman who is divorced, any helpful superstition to ensure a happy marriage is readily accepted by a bride. While a man can easily re-marry, a woman finds it difficult, if not impossible. So, for good luck, a new bride is given a piece of bread dough after the wedding reception by her friends and in-laws. She sticks the dough to the top of the door of her home in the belief that it will bring prosperity and long life to the marriage.

PEPPER PIES
(FATAYER BE FLEFLEH)

I red sweet pepper, *diced*
I green pepper, *diced*
I medium onion, *chopped*
3 tbs lemon juice
I tbl olive oil
I tsp thyme
½ Basic Pie Dough
(see page 26)

1. Mix all the ingredients except the dough.

2. Roll the dough balls ⅛-inch thick; flute the edge by pinching it with your finger and thumb.

3. Spread a tablespoon of the filling on individual rounds, pressing the filling with the spoon. Place the pies on a greased pan. Bake in a 375° oven for 20 minutes or until the dough is golden.

Yields 20 pies

Nutrient value per pie:

Calories	90
Fat	I gram
Cholesterol	0 milligrams
Fiber	0.5 grams
Sodium	10 milligrams

CHEESE AND TOMATO PIES
(FATAYER BEL JEBNEH)

½ lb feta cheese
I cup chopped onion
I cup diced tomato
I tsp oregano
½ Basic Pie Dough
(see page 26)

1. Mix all the ingredients together except the dough.

2. Roll the dough balls into a ⅛-inch thick round loaf. Place a tablespoon of the filling on the rounds and close, shaping each one as a triangle.

3. Place the pies in a greased pan. Bake in a 375° oven until golden.

Yields 20 pies

Nutrient value per pie:

Calories	115
Fat	2 grams
Cholesterol	10 milligrams
Fiber	1.5 grams
Sodium	130 milligrams

RED PEPPER AND SESAME PIES
(FATAYER BEL SEMSUM WEL FLEFLEH)

1 red bell pepper
1 chili pepper
¼ cup sesame seeds
1 cup chopped onion
2 tbs pomegranate molasses
½ Basic Pie Dough
(see page 26)

1. Chop the peppers very finely and mix them with the rest of the ingredients except the dough.

2. Roll the dough balls ⅛-inch thick; flute the edge by pinching it between your finger and thumb.

3. Spread a tablespoon of the filling on individual rounds, pressing the filling with the spoon. Place the pies on a greased pan. Bake at 375° for 15 minutes or until the dough is golden.

Nutrient value per pie:

Calories	107
Fat	1 gram
Cholesterol	0
Fiber	0.6 gram
Sodium	10 milligrams

Yields 20 pies

YOGURT PIES
(FATAYER BEL LABNEH)

1 cup Yogurt Cream Cheese
(see page 98)
2 cups finely chopped onion
1 cup diced tomato, *drained*
1 tbl dry mint
1 tbl oregano
½ Basic Pie Dough
(see page 26)

1. Roll dough into ⅛-inch thick rounds. Flute the edge by pinching between your finger and thumb.

2. Mix all the other ingredients. Evenly spread one teaspoon of the filling onto the individual rounds.

3. Place the pies on a greased pan. Bake at 375° for 15 minutes until the edges are golden.

Nutrient value per pie:

Calories | 120
Fat | less then one gram
Cholesterol | 10 milligrams
Fiber | 0.5 gram
Sodium | 115 milligrams

Yields 20 pies

"Contentment is an inexhaustible treasure."

CHEESE AND PARSLEY PIES
(FATAYER BEL JEBNEH WAL BAYD)

½ lb feta cheese
I cup egg substitute
2 cups chopped parsley
I tsp black pepper
½ Basic Pie Dough
(see page 26)

Nutrient value per pie:

Calories	115
Fat	2 grams
Cholesterol	10 milligrams
Fiber	0.2 gram
Sodium	128 milligrams

1. Beat the egg substitute and mix in with the cheese. Add the parsley and pepper.

2. Roll the dough into circular loaves ⅛-inch thick. Flute the edge by pinching between finger and thumb.

3. Evenly spread a heaping teaspoon of the filling on the individual rounds, pressing gently with the spoon. Bring about ½-inch of the edges up and fold slightly to make a ridge.

4. Place the rounds together on a greased pan. Bake at 375° for 10 to 15 minutes, or until the cheese melts and the edges of the pies are golden.

Yields 20 pies

"I would prefer a smile to welcome me to your home than a good meal."
—Anonymous

SPINACH PIES
(FATAYER BEL SABANEKH)

2 lbs fresh spinach
2 tbs salt
2 medium onion, *chopped*
1 tbl olive oil
½ cup lemon juice
1 tbl sumac
1 cup pomegranate seeds,
optional
½ Basic Pie Dough Recipe
(see page 26)

Nutrient value per pie:

Calories   95
Fat   less then one gram
Cholesterol   0
Fiber   0.8 gram
Sodium   18 milligrams

1. Wash the spinach thoroughly, then chop it. Sprinkle the chopped spinach with salt. Let it stand for 15 minutes, then squeeze out the excess moisture. Mix the spinach with the rest of the ingredients.

2. Roll out the pie dough to 4-inch circles. Put on a heaping tablespoon of the filling. Fold up the bottom to the middle and bring in the sides to center, squeezing them all shut to form a triangle. Bake in a preheated 375° oven until the pies are golden.

Yields 40 pies

31

YOGURT CREAM CHEESE SPREAD
(LEBNEH WA BUSSELL)

I cup Yogurt Cream Cheese
(see page 98)
I cup chopped onion
½ tsp red pepper
I tsp nigella, *optional*
2 tbs chopped walnuts

Nutrient value per serving:

Calories   45
Fat   2 grams
Cholesterol I milligram
Fiber   0.6 gram
Sodium   30 milligrams

I. Mix the cream cheese with the onion, red pepper, and nigella.

2. Serve on a flat dish. Sprinkle with the chopped walnuts.

Yields 6 servings

"Not every white thing is a cheese nor every dark object a raisin."

BULGUR AND YOGURT SPREAD
(KESHEK KHADRA)

1 quart nonfat yogurt
1 cup #1 bulgur wheat
½ cup chopped onion
pepper to taste
¼ cup chopped walnuts

1. Mix the yogurt and the bulgur, cover and let stand for 12 hours.

2. Mix it with the chopped onions and season with pepper. Serve in a flat dish. Sprinkle with the chopped walnuts.

Yields 8 servings

Nutrient value per serving:

Calories	100
Fat	2 grams
Cholesterol	1 milligram
Fiber	3.5 grams
Sodium	25 milligrams

HUMMUS

3 cups cooked chickpeas
2 tbs tahini
¼ lemon juice
¼ cup nonfat yogurt
1 tbl ground cumin

1. Put the cooked chickpeas and two tablespoons of water into a blender. Blend for about 3 minutes. Add the remaining ingredients and blend, stopping a few times to stir until the mixture has turned to a smooth paste. In the Arab world, hummus is served in a shallow dish, sprinkled with paprika and black pepper, and covered with olive oil.

Yields 6 servings

Nutrient value per serving:

Calories	170
Fat	5 grams
Cholesterol	0
Fiber	5 grams
Sodium	12 milligrams

POTATO WITH CORIANDER
(BATATA BEL-KUZBRA)

2 large potatoes
1 tbl ground coriander
1 tbl olive oil
1 tsp black pepper

1. Boil the potatoes until tender, but still somewhat firm. Skin them, and cut them into 1-inch cubes.

2. Sauté the cubes in the oil and add the coriander and pepper. Cook them over low heat for 5 minutes.

Yields 4 servings

Nutrient value per serving:

Calories	145
Fat	4 grams
Cholesterol	0
Fiber	2.5 grams
Sodium	10 milligrams

PRODUCE PEDDLERS

A donkey pulls a cart for the fruit and vegetable peddlers who meander through neighborhoods, singing in order to attract the attention of housewives. Each vegetable has its own song and is given a nickname by the peddler. A housewife, when she hears the nickname of the vegetable she wants, begins negotiating with the peddler from her balcony. When a price is finally agreed upon, the housewife lowers down the money in a basket with a rope, and the peddler exchanges the vegetables and fruit for the money. The vegetables' nicknames vary from village to village; this makes it difficult, at first, for newcomers to buy their produce.

EGGPLANT SPREAD WITH TAHINI
(MUTABEL BAZENJAN)

2 1-lb eggplants
3 cloves garlic, *mashed*
2 tbs lemon juice
¼ cup nonfat yogurt
2 tbs tahini

Nutrient value per serving:

Calories	110
Fat	4 grams
Cholesterol	0
Fiber	4 grams
Sodium	16 milligrams

1. Pierce the eggplant in a few places. To get the best smoked flavor, place on a charcoal grill, turning so that all sides are charred. To broil in an oven, cut the eggplant in half lengthwise. Pierce the skin in a few places. Place the cut side down in a shallow broiler pan. Place the broiler pan about 3 inches from the broiler flame. Broil until the skin begins to blister and the pulp is soft. Remove and peel the skin as soon as the eggplant cools.

2. Mash the eggplant to a smooth puree. Mix the rest of the ingredients, and blend into the eggplant. Refrigerate the mixture. It will taste better when cooled. The spread is usually served in a shallow dish, garnished with pomegranate seeds and chopped parsley.

Yields 4 servings

EGGPLANT SPREAD
(BABA GHANNOUJ)

2 1-lb eggplants
½ cup green bell pepper,
finely chopped
½ cup red bell pepper,
finely chopped
½ cup parsley,
finely chopped
¼ cup lemon juice

1. Broil the eggplants as in the previous recipe, or, for a smoky taste, grill them. Peel the skin and mash the pulp. Mix all ingredients and refrigerate. The spread is usually served in a shallow dish, and sprinkled lightly with olive oil and pomegranate seeds as garnish.

Yields 4 servings

Nutrient value per serving:

Calories	70
Fat	less then one gram
Cholesterol	0
Fiber	6.3 grams
Sodium	15 milligrams

NEIGHBORHOOD

Food peddlers, selling their wares from carts can be found in most Eastern Mediterranean villages and cities. These carts usually appear in the afternoon, remaining until late evening. Because in our part of the world everything must be freshly picked, the food peddlers sell only what food is in season. Wintertime brings freshly roasted chestnuts and peanuts. In the spring, some sell a very sweet blackberry syrup mixed with crushed ice. Others sell fresh green almonds and a special kind of sour plum. In the summer they may sell boiled lupin beans, wrapped in paper and sprinkled with a mixture of salt and cumin. Others sell pistachios, but the two most

SPICY MUSHROOMS
(FITR HAR)

1 lb small fresh mushrooms
1 medium onion, *finely chopped*
1 tbl olive oil
6 cloves garlic, *minced*
½ red bell pepper, *finely chopped*
1 tsp red chili pepper
½ tsp black pepper
1 cup chopped cilantro

1. Boil about 4 cups of water. Drop in the mushrooms and cook for two minutes. Remove them from the water and drain.

2. Sauté the onions in the oil until they are transparent. Add the mushrooms, the garlic, and both peppers. Cook for 5 minutes. Season with black pepper and cilantro. Simmer for another 5 minutes. Serve in a flat dish.

Yields 4 servings

Nutrient value per serving:

Calories	90
Fat	4 grams
Cholesterol	0
Fiber	2.7 grams
Sodium	10 milligrams

FOOD PEDDLERS

popular products are corn and cactus fruit. The corn vender has a cart that is about three cubic feet with a large opening on top. The opening has in it a huge container that can hold up to 200 ears of corn and water in which to boil the corn. A gas stove sits under the container. The peddler begins boiling the corn early in the afternoon so it will be ready for the early crowd of evening strollers. A cactus peddler takes a corner of a busy street, decorates the wall where he is set up with rugs and several pots of colorful flowers. He arranges the cactus fruit on big chunks of ice. When he is ready to sell, he plays Syrian folk music on a tape player.

EGGPLANT WITH EGG
(BAZENJAN BEL BAYD)

2 1-lb eggplants
3 cloves garlic, *mashed*
1 tbl olive oil
½ cup egg substitute
½ tsp black pepper

Nutrient value per serving:

Calories	105
Fat	4 grams
Cholesterol	0
Fiber	5.7 grams
Sodium	50 milligrams

1. Grill or broil eggplants as described in the Eggplant Spread recipe on page 35.

2. Mash the pulp.

3. Sauté the garlic in the oil over medium heat for no more than 1 minute, then add the eggplant and cook it for 3 minutes.

4. Whisk the egg substitute; add it and the black pepper to the eggplant. Continue to cook for 5 minutes, stirring occasionally.

Yields 4 servings

CHICKPEAS WITH TAHINI SAUCE
(MOUSABAHA)

3 cups chickpeas
1½ cups Cumin-Yogurt Sauce (see page 78)

Nutrient value per serving:

Calories	175
Fat	3 grams
Cholesterol	0
Fiber	5 grams
Sodium	20 milligrams

1. Drain the beans and put them in a deep dish. Pour the sauce on top of the garbanzo beans.

Yields 6 servings

FALAFEL

Falafel sandwiches are the stuff that drove many an Arab mother to distraction. When I was in school in Syria, I would buy a falafel sandwich on the way home in the afternoons, then proclaim no appetite when my mother offered the evening meal. At parties, falafel is served on mini-pita loaves, with its condiments of chopped onion mixed with sumac, sliced tomatoes, pickled turnips, and tahini sauce.

1 lb dry chickpeas
1 medium onion
1 cup chopped parsley
1 cup chopped cilantro
1 tbl ground coriander
1 tbl cumin
½ tsp black pepper
1 tbl baking powder

Nutrient value per patty when baked:

Calories 25
Fat less then one gram
Cholesterol 0
Fiber 0.9 gram
Sodium 20 milligrams

1. Soak the beans in cold water for 24 hours. Mix all the ingredients except the baking powder. Grind the mixture in a food processor until it turns to a thick paste. Add the baking powder and let the mixture set for 30 minutes, then shape into patties.

2. Traditionally, falafel are deep-fried in olive oil, but I broil them in the oven, which drastically cuts the number of calories. I must admit, however, that they taste better when fried.

Yields 40 small patties

VEGETARIAN STUFFED GRAPE LEAVES
(WARAQ INAB)

Stuffed grape leaves, zucchini, and eggplant appear among the many *mazza* dishes. They are also popular main dishes. Smaller vegetables—often no more than two bites apiece—filled with light stuffings are used for appetizers, while bigger vegetables with stuffings that often include meat are the choice for main dishes.

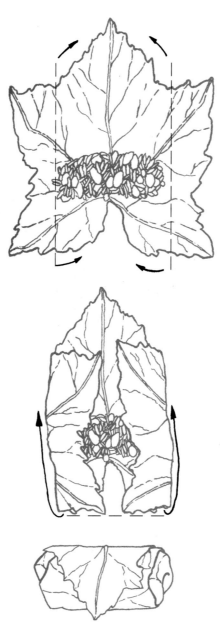

2 medium onions,
finely chopped
1 tbl olive oil
1½ cups rice
4 cups water
2 large tomatoes,
finely chopped
1 cup chopped parsley
8 cloves garlic, *minced*
½ cup lemon juice
1 tbl allspice
½ tsp black pepper
1-lb fresh vine leaves or
1 16-oz can vine leaves
1-2 large potatoes or
onions, *sliced*

Nutrient value per serving:

Calories	180
Fat	2 grams
Cholesterol	0
Fiber	3 grams
Sodium	100 milligrams

1. In a pan, sauté the onions in the olive oil until transparent. Add the rice and 1 cup of water. Cook for 5 minutes. Now, combine the rice mixture with the rest of the ingredients except the sliced potatoes or onions, grape leaves, and remaining water. Mix well.

2. Pour hot water over the fresh vine leaves and set aside for 10 minutes. If you are using the canned leaves, wash them in water, drain, then set aside.

3. Put 1 tablespoon of the stuffing in the center of the rough side of each leaf. Fold the stem side horizontally over the stuffing, then fold the 2 vertical sides over the first fold; roll tightly until it reaches the leaf point, forming a cylinder 3 inches long by 1 inch thick. What's important is that you fold the ends in before rolling so the stuffing does not come out. (See picture.)

4. Cover the bottom of the pan with potato or onion slices to prevent the grape leaves from sticking to the bottom. For each layer, place the rolls side by side. On top of the final layer place a round, flat plate, and press lightly to prevent the rolls from loosening while cooking. Add the rest of the water; it should be enough to cover the leaves. Cook over low heat for ½ hour; then simmer for another hour.

5. Remove and add more lemon juice if desired. Unmold on a round shallow platter. This dish is served at room temperature, so it can be prepared well in advance of serving.

Yields 10 servings

STUFFED ZUCCHINI
(MEHSHEE KUSA BEL ZEYT)

6 small zucchini, *cored*
I cup rice
4 cloves of garlic, *mashed*
I medium onion, *finely chopped*
½ cup chopped parsley
I large ripe tomato, *finely chopped*
I tbl olive oil
½ tsp black pepper
½ tsp allspice
4 large tomatoes, *sliced*
4 cups water

Nutrient value per zucchini:

Calories	195
Fat	3 grams
Cholesterol	0
Fiber	5.8 grams
Sodium	100 milligrams

I. Combine the rice, mashed garlic, the onions, parsley, the chopped tomatoes, the olive oil, and half of the pepper and allspice. Mix well. Stuff the zucchini ¾ full with the mixture.

2. In a large, deep cooking pot, layer the zucchini, arranged with the sliced tomatoes. Add the water, using enough to cover the zucchini, half the pepper, and allspice. Bring it to boil, then simmer for 30-40 minutes, or until the zucchini is tender.

3. Arrange the stuffed zucchini in a shallow serving plate.

Yields 6 servings

*"Approach food only when you desire it.
Stop eating while the desire is still there."*
—The Prophet Mohammad

STUFFED ITALIAN EGGPLANTS
(MEHSHEE BATENJAN BEL ZEYT)

This recipe calls for the long, slender Italian eggplant, not the large, bulbous sort.

6 Italian eggplants
1 cup rice
1 medium onion, *finely chopped*
1 tbl olive oil
1 large ripe tomato, *finely chopped*
4 large tomatoes, *sliced*
4 gloves garlic, *mashed*
4 cups water
½ tsp black pepper

1. Combine the rice, garlic, the onion, the chopped tomatoes, olive oil, and half the seasoning of black pepper. Mix well. Stuff the eggplants ¾ full with the mixture.

2. In a large, deep cooking pot, layer the eggplant, arranged with the sliced tomatoes. Add the water and remaining pepper. Bring to a boil, then simmer for 30-40 minutes or until the eggplants are tender.

3. Arrange the stuffed eggplant in a shallow serving plate.

Yields 6 servings

Nutrient value per eggplant:

Calories	200
Fat	3 grams
Cholesterol	0
Fiber	9 grams
Sodium	100 milligrams

"It is said that people eat with their eyes, so make the food look good."
—Anonymous

SWISS CHARD WITH TAHINI
(SELEK BEL TAHINI)

1 lb Swiss chard
¼ cup lemon juice
3-4 cloves garlic, *minced*
2 tbs tahini

1. Cut the Swiss chard into small pieces. Bring water to a boil in a deep pan. Drop the cut Swiss chard into the boiling water, and cook for about 5 minutes. Drain the Swiss chard, and squeeze the excess water.

2. Blend the lemon juice with the garlic, tahini, and half a cup of water. Mix the Swiss chard with the sauce, and correct the seasoning.

Nutrient value per serving:

Calories	75
Fat	4 grams
Cholesterol	0
Fiber	2.6 grams
Sodium	250 milligrams

Yields 4 servings

ZUCCHINI IN POMEGRANATE MOLASSES
(KUSA BE DEBS AL-RUMAN)

1 lb zucchini
¼ cup pomegranate molasses
1 red bell pepper, *finely chopped*
4 cloves garlic, *minced*

1. Cook the zucchini in water for about 20 minutes, or until they are tender. Drain the water, and mash the zucchini. Let it sit for 5 minutes, then scoop off the excess water.

2. Mix the pomegranate molasses with the chopped bell pepper and the garlic. Fold into the mashed zucchini, and adjust the seasoning.

Nutrient value per serving:

Calories	60
Fat	less then one gram
Cholesterol	0
Fiber	2.6 grams
Sodium	6 milligrams

Yields 4 servings

SWEET AND SOUR BEET DIP
(SHAMANDER BEL TAHINI)

This pink dip adds a lively splash of color to the table.

4 beets
1 tbl tahini
2 cloves garlic, *minced*
¼ cup lemon juice
¼ cup nonfat yogurt

1. Boil and peel the beets, then mash them.

2. Mix the tahini with the lemon juice, garlic, and the yogurt. Fold in the mashed beets; blend well.

Yields 4 servings

Nutrient value per serving:

Calories	60
Fat	2 grams
Cholesterol	0
Fiber	1.3 grams
Sodium	55 milligrams

استكبِرْها ولو كانت عجزة

"Choose it large, though not yet ripe."

45

RED PEPPER SPREAD
(MUHAMARA)

This appetizer is particular to Aleppo, Syria. If it's found anywhere else, you can bet that it originated in Aleppo, where piquant tastes are appreciated.

3 slices whole wheat bread
1½ red bell pepper
¼ cup walnuts
1 medium onion
1 tbl ground coriander
1 tbl ground cumin
¼ cup pomegranate molasses
½ to 1 red chili pepper,
to taste
pomegranate seeds for
garnish

1. Put all the ingredients, including the bread, in a food processor and blend until you get a smooth paste. Serve in a flat dish and garnish with fresh pomegranate seeds.

Yields 8 servings

Nutrient value per serving:

Calories	100
Fat	3 grams
Cholesterol	0
Fiber	2 grams
Sodium	60 milligrams

Chapter Five
Salads

Whenever I order a salad in an American restaurant, no matter how exotic its name, invariably I'm served a pile of lettuce—most of the time iceberg lettuce—and a tomato slice or two, and, if I'm lucky, a cucumber slice and shredded carrots. I asked a friend why this should be a typical American salad. Her answer was, "Americans don't fill up on salads, we save our appetites for the good stuff."

"The good stuff?" I asked, "what good stuff? The butter, the meat and the rich sauces?"

By all means, fill up on salads if you can. You'll live longer. When vegetables are cooked, they lose a lot of essential nutrients, especially water-soluble vitamins. It's a good idea to eat as much salad as you can, loaded with as many vegetables as possible. Depending on what else you eat, a salad may be your only source of vitamins and minerals for the day. There is little dispute that eating more fiber, such as salad greens, cuts the risk of intestinal and colon cancer. Dark green or dark-orange vegetables and fruits are high in beta-carotene, which is believed to decrease the risk of breast and skin cancer. Vegetables, legumes (beans), and grains, such as bulgar wheat and rice, move rapidly through the digestive system. Red meat and whole milk dairy products, such as cheese, sit for long periods in the intestine, exposing us to all the chemicals that people pump into livestock before they are butchered or milked. Hence, the increased risk of colon and intestinal cancer.

One positive development in America and Europe in the past couple of decades is the addition of fast food salad bars as a supplement, or even as an alternative, to fat-filled hamburgers and greasy french fries.

In the Levant, a salad is part of virtually every meal, even breakfast. Although most Levantine salad ingredients vary, the dressing—olive oil and lemon juice—remains the same. Always remember to mix the dressing with the vegetables just before serving. Doing so keeps the salad ingredients fresher longer.

Tabbouli is a famous salad and one of the basic items in the mazza. Making tabbouli is especially popular as a group project among women in the Levant. Tabbouli requires a great deal of chopping, particularly of the parsley into an extra fine chaff. At times, making tabbouli becomes a social occasion for women, who invite each other under the pretense that it will be a tabbouli-making event. Keep in mind, however, that they chop at least ten bunches of parsley for each salad.

One of the folk songs I learned from my mother deals with making tabbouli:

Mashghuli mashghuli
Am ba'amel tabbouli
Jhay la andna 'l asmar
Oo'l laili tah niss har
Sahra mahouli

It rhymes in Arabic, so forgive the lack of rhyme or rhythm in this loose translation:

> I'm busy, I'm busy
> I'm making tabbouli
> Our brunette friend
> Will visit tonight
> And we're going to have
> A big party

Here are the recipes for tabbouli and other delicious and healthy salads:

TABBOULI

½ cup #2 bulgur wheat
½ cup water
4 cups finely chopped ripe tomatoes
½ cup fresh lemon juice
2 tbs olive oil
2 large bunches parsley, *about 5 cups finely chopped*
1 cup chopped onions
1 tbl dried mint flakes

Nutrient value per serving:

Calories	110
Fat	5 grams
Cholesterol	0
Fiber	3.8 grams
Sodium	40 milligrams

1. Rinse the bulgur, drain, then add ½ cup of the water and let stand for 15 minutes. Place the bulgur in a large mixing bowl, then add the tomatoes and lemon juice. Chop the parsley. Place on top of the bulgur and tomato mixture. Add onion, mint flakes, and the oil and mix thoroughly.

2. Tabbouli can be prepared a couple hours ahead of time if you wish. Simply leave out the oil and lemon juice dressing until you're ready to serve. Adding the dressing too soon makes the parsley wilt and creates too much liquid in the bottom of the salad bowl.

3. In the Arab world, tabbouli is scooped up and eaten with lettuce leaves, rather than with silverware. Putting each serving of tabbouli inside a lettuce or a cabbage leaf rather than displaying them in a flat dish is a very tempting presentation. Or, for an elegant looking and tasting *hors d'oeuvre*, cut cherry tomatoes in half, remove the center, and fill them with tabbouli.

Yields 6 servings

PITA BREAD SALAD
(FETTOUSH)

Fettoush was created as a way to use up stale and dry bread. Nowadays, fresh pita bread is toasted to dry it out before adding it to the salad.

I large loaf pita bread
8 large leaves romaine lettuce
I cup chopped parsley
I small green pepper
I cucumber, *peeled and cut into ½-inch slices*
3 medium tomatoes, *cut into I-inch cubes*
8 radishes, *cut into ½-inch slices*
4 green onions, *cut into ¼-inch slices*
I small onion, *sliced*
I clove garlic, *mashed*
I tbl sumac
I tbl oregano
I tbl dried mint
I tbl olive oil
I cup lemon juice

1. Toast the pita bread in the oven until golden brown, and then break into I-inch pieces.

2. In the salad bowl, tear lettuce into small pieces as you would for a tossed green salad. Add the chopped pepper, cucumber, tomatoes, radishes, onion, and the toasted bread.

3. In a small bowl mix the mashed garlic with the rest of the ingredients to make the dressing. Mix the dressing just before serving to avoid making the bread mushy.

Yields 8 servings

Nutrient value per serving:

Calories	90
Fat	2 grams
Cholesterol	0
Fiber	2.3 grams
Sodium	75 milligrams

TOMATO SALAD
(SALATAT BANADOURA)

This salad is especially good with *Mjadara* and other bulgur, rice, and legume dishes.

1 clove garlic
¼ cup lemon juice
1 tbl olive oil
1 tbl dry mint
4 tomatoes
1 medium sweet onion, *chopped*

1. Mash garlic in a bowl. Add the lemon juice, olive oil, and mint, then mix well. Cut the tomatoes into bite-size pieces and place in a serving dish. Add the onion and the lemon dressing and serve.

Yields 4 servings

Nutrient value per serving:

Calories	75
Fat	4 grams
Cholesterol	0
Fiber	2 grams
Sodium	15 milligrams

"Feed the mouth, close the eyes"

POTATO SALAD
(SALATAT BATATA)

Levantine potato salad is very different, and much tastier and healthier than the mayonnaise-based potato salad of American delis.

4 potatoes
1 cup chopped parsley
1 cup chopped onion
2 cups diced tomatoes
2 tbs olive oil
¼ cup lemon juice
1 tsp pepper

1. Boil and peel potaoes.

2. Cut the potatoes into 1-inch pieces. Mix the potatoes with the rest of the ingredients and serve.

Yields 6 servings

Nutrient value per serving:

Calories	143
Fat	5 grams
Cholesterol	0
Fiber	3 grams
Sodium	15 milligrams

CRAVEN

A pregnant woman's cravings in Syrian villages usually create a buzz of activity among the neighbors. In addition to considering it an honor to help a neighbor who is pregnant, there is a bit of Middle East voodoo involved. A belief is afoot that if the expectant mother does not get what she craves, the shape of that craving will appear as a birthmark on the baby, precisely on the spot that the mother scratches at the time of the craving. And so it happens that if a baby's birthmark looks like

MIXED SALAD
(SALATA MSHAKLEH)

1 clove garlic
¼ cup lemon juice
2 tbs olive oil
pepper to taste
1 bell pepper
8 leaves romaine lettuce
3 spring onions
1 medium cucumber
2 medium tomatoes
4 radishes
1 carrot
½ cup chopped parsley
¼ cup chopped mint

1. Mash the garlic, and then add the lemon juice, olive oil, and black pepper; mix well. Cut all vegetables into bite-size pieces. When ready to serve, add the dressing to the vegetables and toss thoroughly.

Yields 6 servings

Nutrient value per serving:

Calories	84
Fat	4.5 grams
Cholesterol	0
Fiber	3 grams
Sodium	80 milligrams

CRAVING

cherries, the neighborhood is convinced that the mother craved cherries, whether or not she admits to it.

There is a certain advantage for expectant mothers in this myth. A wife who understands the fear caused by it will begin by asking her husband for everything she craves. It is at his—and his future child's—peril if he refuses to scour the village for strange and unusual food.

YOGURT AND CUCUMBER SALAD
(SALATAT LABAN BE KHYAR)

2 cloves garlic
2 tbs of dry mint
1½ cup water
3 cups nonfat yogurt
2 cups chopped cucumbers

1. In a mixing bowl, mash the garlic, then add the mint flakes and water. Add this mix to the yogurt and stir well until no lumps are left. Add the chopped cucumber to the yogurt mix and serve.

Yields 4 servings

Nutrient value per serving:

Calories 100
Fat less then one gram
Cholesterol 4 milligrams
Fiber 0.5 gram
Sodium 135 milligrams

WATERCRESS SALAD
(SALATAT AL-JARJEER)

2 bunches watercress, *chopped*
1 cup chopped sweet onion
2 cups sliced mushrooms
¼ cup lemon juice
1 tbl olive oil

1. Mix all ingredients together and serve.

Yields 4 servings

Nutrient value per serving:

Calories 70
Fat 4 grams
Cholesterol 0
Fiber 3.8 grams
Sodium 50 milligrams

CHICKPEA SALAD
(SALATAT HUMMUS)

2 cups chickpeas,
cooked and drained
1 green bell pepper
1 red bell pepper
1 yellow bell pepper
½ tsp crushed hot red
pepper
2 tbs lemon juice
1 tbl olive oil
1 tsp ground black pepper

1. Chop the peppers.
2. Mix all ingredients and serve.

Yields 4 servings

Nutrient value per serving:

Calories	260
Fat	6 grams
Cholesterol	0
Fiber	6 grams
Sodium	10 milligrams

CHICKPEA AND CUMIN SALAD
(SALATAT HUMMUS BEL KAMMOUN)

3 cups chickpeas,
cooked and drained
1 cup parsley, *chopped*
1 cup Cumin-Yogurt Sauce
(see page 78)
2 tbs dry mint
¼ tsp red pepper

1. Combine the beans and the parsley in a bowl. Pour the Cumin-Yogurt Sauce over the chickpeas. Add the pepper and mix.

Yields 4 servings

Nutrient value per serving:

Calories	250
Fat	3 grams
Cholesterol	0
Fiber	9 grams
Sodium	30 milligrams

LENTIL SALAD
(SALATAT ADAS)

3 cups cooked lentils
1 cup chopped sweet onions
½ cup green bell pepper,
finely chopped
¼ cup red bell pepper,
finely chopped
¼ cup lemon juice
1 tbl olive oil
1 tsp ground cumin
1 tsp ground sage

1. Mix the lentils, onions, and peppers. For the dressing, mix the rest of the ingredients, then pour over the vegetables. Mix and serve.

Yields 4 servings

Nutrient value per serving:

Calories	230
Fat	4 grams
Cholesterol	0
Fiber	13 grams
Sodium	10 milligrams

"When you interfere between the onion and its skin, only a bad smell will result."
(Stay out of other people's arguments.)
—Anonymous

CABBAGE SALAD
(SALATAT MALFOUF)

2 cups chopped green
cabbage leaves
I cup chopped red cabbage
I cup chopped sweet onions
I cup grated carrots
¼ cup lemon juice
I tbl olive oil

I. Place the chopped green and red cabbage in a bowl. Add the onions and the carrots; mix. Whisk together the remaining ingredients and pour over the vegetables.

Yields 4 servings

Nutrient value per serving:

Calories	70
Fat	4 grams
Cholesterol	0
Fiber	2.6 grams
Sodium	20 milligrams

RADISH AND CABBAGE SALAD
(SALATAT FEJEL WA MALFOUF)

3 cups sliced radishes
2 cups chopped
green cabbage
½ cup sliced onion
¼ cup lemon juice
I tbl olive oil
¼ tsp ground black pepper

I. Mix the radishes, cabbage, and onion in a bowl. Whisk the lemon juice, olive oil, and pepper. Pour the dressing over the vegetables and mix.

Yields 4 servings

Nutrient value per serving:

Calories	65
Fat	4 grams
Cholesterol	0
Fiber	2.7 grams
Sodium	30 milligrams

CUCUMBER AND RADISH SALAD
(SALATAT KHYAR WA FEJEL)

3 cups sliced radishes

2 pickling cucumbers, *sliced thin*

1 tbl olive oil

2 tbs lemon juice

1. Place the radishes and cucumbers in a shallow serving bowl. Prepare the dressing by mixing together the olive oil and lemon juice. Pour the dressing over the vegetables just before serving.

Yields 4 servings

Nutrient value per serving:

Calories	60
Fat	4 grams
Cholesterol	0
Fiber	2 grams
Sodium	25 milligrams

MUSHROOM SALAD
(SALATAT FITR)

4 cups sliced mushrooms

1 cup sliced sweet onion

1 cup chopped parsley

½ cup lemon juice

1 tbl olive oil

1 tsp thyme

1. Mix all the ingredients together and serve.

Yields 4 servings

Nutrient value per serving:

Calories	75
Fat	4 grams
Cholesterol	0
Fiber	2 grams
Sodium	15 milligrams

BULGUR WHEAT SALAD
(SAFF)

1 cup dry chickpeas
1 cup #1 bulgur wheat
1 cup cold water
2 cups chopped tomatoes
1 cup chopped sweet onion
1 cup chopped cucumber
⅔ cup lemon juice
1 tbl dry mint flakes
1 tbl olive oil
½ tsp pepper

1. Soak the chickpeas in water overnight, then remove their skin and split into halves by placing them in a plastic bag and rolling them with a rolling pin.

2. Place the bulgur wheat in bowl, stir in water and leave to soak for an hour.

3. Add the chickpeas and the rest of the vegetables to the bulgur wheat and mix. Whisk together the lemon juice, mint flakes, olive oil, and pepper. Pour the dressing over the mixed vegetables and stir.

Yields 6 servings

Nutrient value per serving:

Calories	365
Fat	4 grams
Cholesterol	0
Fiber	15 grams
Sodium	30 milligrams

> *"The stomach is the source of sickness.*
> *Good diet is the prevention."*
> —Anonymous

SALADS

SPINACH SALAD
(SALATAT SABANEKH)

1 lb spinach
2 tbs chopped walnuts, *optional*
1 cup chopped onion
1 cup pomegranate seeds
2 cloves garlic, *mashed*
¼ cup lemon juice
¼ tsp red pepper
1 tbl olive oil

Nutrient value per serving:

Calories	125
Fat	6 grams
Cholesterol	0
Fiber	4 grams
Sodium	95 milligrams

1. Prepare the spinach by washing thoroughly, rinsing, towel drying, and coarsely chopping it. Place it in a paper towel and refrigerate until just before serving. Place the walnuts on a cookie sheet and bake in a 275° oven for 12 to 15 minutes, stirring occasionally until they are lightly toasted. Put the spinach in a large salad bowl; add the onion and the pomegranate seeds. Whisk together the garlic, lemon juice, pepper, and the olive oil. Just before serving, stir in the toasted walnuts and mix the dressing.

Yields 4 servings

HERB SALAD
(SALATAT BAHARAT)

2 cups fresh oregano leaves
1 cup fresh thyme
1 cup scallions, *chopped*
1 cup tomato, *chopped*
1 tbl olive oil
1 tsp sumac
2 tbs lemon juice

Nutrient value per serving:

Calories	50
Fat	4 grams
Cholesterol	0
Fiber	1.2 grams
Sodium	10 milligrams

1. Mix all the ingredients together and serve.

Yields 4 servings

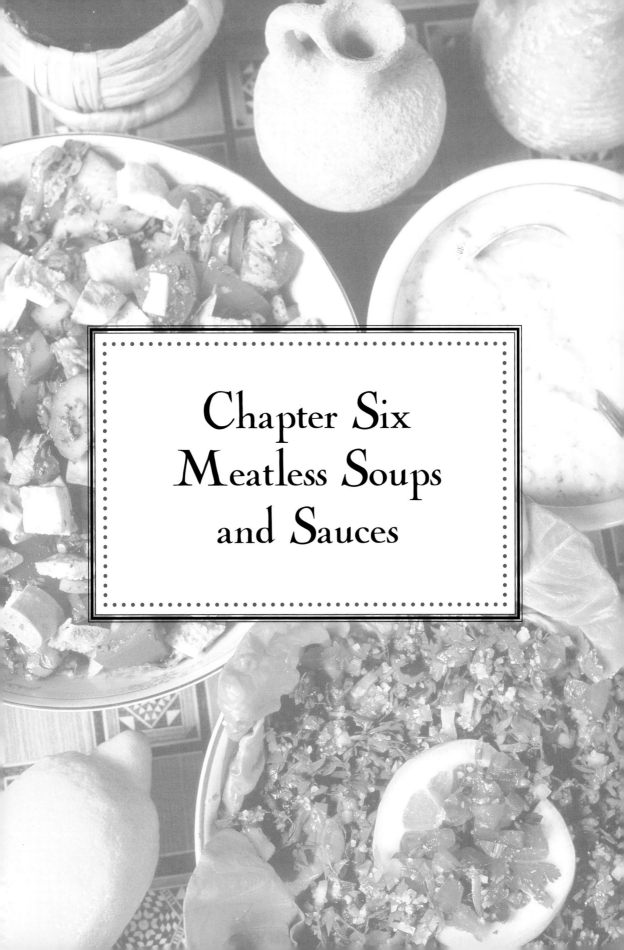

Chapter Six
Meatless Soups
and Sauces

Most of the soups in this section are low in fat and calories, yet filling enough to serve as a full luncheon meal. You can omit even the small amount of oil called for in these recipes if you are required to cook no-fat meals. By including the spices and herbs recommended here, you won't miss the oil.

Some cooks substitute vegetable or chicken stock when oil is omitted from the recipe. I suggest using a heavy cast iron frying pan and using nothing in place of oil.

LENTIL LEMON SOUP
(SHORBET ADAS BEL HAMATH)

2 cups lentils
11 cups water
1 cup chopped onion
pepper to taste
2 cups chopped cilantro
6 cloves garlic, *mashed*
1 tbl olive oil
½ cup lemon juice
½ cup small pasta shell

Nutrient value per serving:

Calories	170
Fat	2 grams
Cholesterol	0
Fiber	9 grams
Sodium	15 milligrams

1. In a cooking pan combine the lentils with the water and onion. Season with pepper. Cook until they are very soft.

2. Mix half the cilantro with mashed garlic, then sauté the mixture in olive oil for no more than 1 minute.

3. When the lentils are soft, add the cilantro and garlic mixture and the lemon juice. Cook for 5 minutes.

4. Now add the pasta to soak up the excess liquid in the pot, and cook until the pasta is done. Sprinkle the soup with the rest of the cilantro before serving.

Yields 10 servings

POTATO SOUP
(SHORBET BATATA)

2 large potatoes
6 cups water
I cup chopped onion
I tbl olive oil
I cup skim milk
I clove of garlic, *mashed*
I bay leaf
I tbl paprika, *optional*
pepper to taste

Nutrient value per serving:

Calories	130
Fat	4 grams
Cholesterol	0
Fiber	2 grams
Sodium	50 milligrams

I. Peel the potatoes, cut into 2-inch pieces, and boil in the water until they are soft. Purée the potatoes and their water in the blender.

2. In a large cooking pan, sauté the onions in the olive oil until tender. Add the puréed potatoes, garlic, milk, bay leaf and paprika (which gives the soup a nice pink color), and cook over low heat for 10 minutes, or until the soup thickens. Discard the bay leaf before serving.

Yields 4 servings

*"There is blessing in three things:
in the early morning meal, in bread
and in soup."*

—*The Prophet Mohammad*

TOMATO SOUP
(SHORBET BANADOURA)

½ chopped onion
1 tbl olive oil
½ cup tomato paste
5 cups water
1 bay leaf
½ tsp thyme
pepper to taste
1 cup angel hair pasta,
broken into 1-inch lengths

1. Sauté the onion in olive oil until tender, then add tomato paste, water, bay leaf, thyme, and pepper. Cover and cook until it begins to boil. Turn the heat to medium and let the soup cook for 5 minutes.

2. Add the pasta and cook until it is done. Do not overcook the pasta. *Al dente*, or a bit crunchy to the bite, is perfect for any kind of pasta.

Nutrient value per serving:

Calories	75
Fat	3 grams
Cholesterol	0
Fiber	1.5 grams
Sodium	200 milligrams

Yields 6 servings

VEGETABLE LENTIL SOUP
(SHORBET ADAS BEL KHUDAR)

1 medium onion
2 tbs olive oil
2 carrots, *peeled and finely chopped*
2 stalks of celery, *finely chopped*
2 ripe tomatoes, *peeled and diced*
2 cups lentils, *washed*
10 cups water
pepper to taste
1 bay leaf

1. Sauté the onions in the olive oil over medium heat until they begin to turn brown. Add the chopped celery, carrots and tomatoes, and cook until they are very soft. If the vegetables start to stick, add some water. Continue adding water and cooking until the celery and carrots are done.

2. Add the lentils, the rest of the water, pepper, and the bay leaf. Allow the mixture to simmer until the lentils are quite soft, probably about 30 minutes. Discard the bay leaf before serving.

Yields 8 servings

Nutrient value per serving:

Calories	220
Fat	4 grams
Cholesterol	0
Fiber	12 grams
Sodium	30 milligrams

LENTIL CREAM SOUP
(SHORBET ADAS MAT-HOON)

1 cup orange split lentils
½ cup rice
6 cups water
1 cup chopped onion
¼ cup chopped cilantro
1 tbl olive oil
1 tbl cumin
pepper to taste

1. Place the lentils and rice in the water and cook for 30 minutes. Sauté the chopped onion and cilantro in the olive oil, then add the mixture to the lentils along with the cumin and pepper. Blend the mixture in a blender, then continue cooking for 10 minutes or until it thickens.

Yields 4 servings

Nutrient value per serving:

Calories	190
Fat	4 grams
Cholesterol	0
Fiber	5 grams
Sodium	15 milligrams

VEGETABLE SOUP
(SHORBET AL KHUDAR)

1 cup chopped onion
1 tbl olive oil
2 celery stalks
2 carrots
1 medium turnip
1 medium tomato
1 medium potato
½ cup tomato paste
1 bay leaf
1 tsp thyme
pepper to taste
8 cups water
1 15-oz can pinto beans

1. Sauté the onions in the olive oil until they are golden. Dice all the vegetables, except the beans, then add them to the onions along with the tomato paste, bay leaf, thyme, and pepper. Sauté for 5 minutes, then add the water and the beans, and cook until all the vegetables are tender. Discard the bay leaf before serving.

Yields 6 servings

Nutrient value per serving:

Calories	170
Fat	3 grams
Cholesterol	0
Fiber	9 grams
Sodium	90 milligrams

HIPPOCRATES,
*the father of medicine, believed that
"your food is your cure."*

MUSHROOM SOUP
(SHORBET AL FITR)

2 potatoes,
peeled & cut into small pieces
6 cups water
½ cup chopped onion
2 cups sliced mushrooms
1 cup red bell pepper,
chopped
1 clove garlic, *mashed*
1 tbl olive oil
1 tsp paprika
½ cup chopped parsley
pepper to taste

1. Start the potatoes and the onion in 6 cups of cold water over high heat and boil until the potatoes are very soft. Purée potatoes and onion and their liquid in a blender. Return to the stove.

2. Cook them over low heat. Sauté the mushrooms, garlic and pepper in the olive oil for couple minutes. Add this mixture, along with the paprika, parsley and pepper to the potatoes and cook for 10 minutes. Sprinkle with chopped parsley.

Yields 4 servings

Nutrient value per serving:

Calories	85
Fat	4 grams
Cholesterol	0
Fiber	2.8 grams
Sodium	290 milligrams

SPLIT PEA SOUP
(SHORBET BAZYLEYA YABSEH)

1½ cup split peas
7 cups water
1 celery stalk
1 medium onion
1 tbl cumin
1 bay leaf
¼ cup lemon juice
pepper to taste

1. Put all the ingredients, except the bay leaf, lemon juice, and pepper, in a slow cooker and cook on high for 5 hours. In a blender, purée the soup. Pour the mixture into a cooking pot, add the bay leaf, lemon juice and pepper, and cook over medium heat for 10 minutes.

Yields 6 servings

Nutrient value per serving:

Calories	190
Fat	1 gram
Cholesterol	0
Fiber	13 grams
Sodium	25 milligrams

صحيح لا تكسر ومكسور لا تاكل وكول تا تشبع

"Whole loaves do not break;
broken pieces do not eat; but consume all you can!"

LENTIL AND SWISS CHARD SOUP
(SHORBET ADAS WA SELEK)

2 cups lentils
10 cups water
1 potato, *diced*
½ lb Swiss chard, *chopped*
1 large onion, *chopped*
4 cloves garlic, *mashed*
1 tbl ground coriander
2 tbs olive oil
2 tbs flour
½ cup lemon juice
pepper to taste

Nutrient value per serving:

Calories	130
Fat	4 grams
Cholesterol	0
Fiber	5 grams
Sodium	75 milligrams

1. Cook the lentils in the water until they are half done—about 15 minutes. Add the diced potato and cook over medium heat for 30 minutes, or until the potatoes are soft. Drop in the chopped Swiss chard and continue to cook for 15 minutes.

2. While the lentils are cooking, brown the chopped onion, mashed garlic, and the coriander in the olive oil. Blend in the flour thoroughly, making sure there are no lumps. Take ½ cup of water from the boiling lentils and add to the mixture to make it easier to stir the flour paste into the soup. Add the lemon juice and pepper, and cook for another 10 minutes.

Yields 8 servings

THREE BEAN SOUP
(SHORBET AL-HBOOB)

8 cups water
1 cup lentils, *washed*
1 cup chopped onion
1 celery stalk, *chopped*
1 clove garlic, *mashed*
1 cup green pepper,
chopped
1 cup red pepper,
chopped
1 tbl olive oil
1 cup cooked chickpeas
1 cup cooked or frozen
black eyed peas
2 cups diced tomatoes

1. Bring the water to boil, add the lentils, and boil them until they are soft. Sauté the onion, celery, garlic, and peppers in the olive oil for 3-4 minutes. Add these vegetables and the rest of the ingredients to the lentils, and continue to cook over medium heat for another 20 minutes.

Yields 8 servings

Nutrient value per serving:

Calories	170
Fat	4 grams
Cholesterol	0
Fiber	8 grams
Sodium	150 milligrams

SAUCES

Sauces are used only in a few recipes as part of the main course. Most of the time, sauces are served as a dip for vegetables and pita chips, a dressing for fish, or as an appetizer.

GARLIC AND OLIVE OIL SAUCE
(TOOM BEL ZEYT)

2 slices white bread, *crust removed*

10 cloves garlic

4 tbl olive oil

½ cup water

Nutrient value per serving:

Calories 65

Fat 6 grams

Cholesterol 0

Fiber 0

Sodium 30 milligrams

1. Soak the bread in water, squeeze and crumble into blender, add the garlic, then purée until the garlic is mashed. Turn the blender on low speed and add the olive oil gradually until the sauce is creamy and pale yellow in color. This sauce is usually served as a dip for grilled meat; it is especially good with grilled chicken. It is delicious, but don't plan on doing much kissing or close-up conversation after you've ingested all this garlic.

Yields 10 servings

During winters in Safsafi, my grandparents had a hole six inches deep and a foot wide, which my grandfather filled with ground-up olive pits left over from pressing olive oil. When lit, the ground pits produced neither flame nor smoke. They only glowed, and gave off a wonderful warmth throughout the night.

GARLIC AND YOGURT SAUCE
(TOOM BEL LABAN)

This is the low-calorie version of the previous sauce, and it is also less strong.

1 tbl cornstarch
2 tbs water
10 cloves garlic
1 cup nonfat yogurt
1 slice white bread, *crust removed*

1. Mix the cornstarch with the water. Put all ingredients in a blender and blend until you get a creamy, white sauce. Serve as an appetizer or as a sauce for grilled meat or chicken.

Yields 10 servings

Nutrient value per serving:

Calories	30
Fat	less then one gram
Cholesterol	0
Fiber	0
Sodium	35 milligrams

GARLIC LEMON SAUCE
(TOOM BEL LIMON)

6 cloves garlic
2 tbl olive oil
½ cup lemon juice
1 tsp black pepper

1. Blend all the ingredients in a blender or food processor until the garlic is mashed. It is served like the previous sauces: with appetizers, grilled or roasted meat, and poultry.

Yields 5 servings

Nutrient value per serving:

Calories	65
Fat	5 grams
Cholesterol	0
Fiber	0
Sodium	5 milligrams

BASIC TAHINI SAUCE
(TARATOUR)

2 cloves garlic
2 tbl tahini
½ cup water
½ cup lemon juice
1 tbl cumin

1. Mash the garlic and blend in the tahini. Gradually add water, lemon juice, and cumin, and continue blending until the sauce becomes smooth. If you prefer a thicker sauce, add less water. This sauce is served with fried or broiled vegetables, and fried or baked fish.

Yields 8 servings

Nutrient value per serving:

Calories 45
Fat 3.5 grams
Cholesterol 0
Fiber less then one gram
Sodium 10 milligrams

THE

A tanoor is a three foot by two foot oven made from a special kind of clay that retains heat. Usually, four to five families will share a tanoor, so it is placed in a location convenient for all the families involved. It is usually placed on the ground next to a wall. The space between the tanoor and the wall is filled with rocks that are packed smoothly with a special clay.

On baking day, the housewife generally mixes enough dough for at least fifty loaves of bread. While the dough is proofing, she lights the firewood in the tanoor. The tanoor is ready for baking when the flame dies down and the wood coals are glowing. Baking in the tanoor is usually a collaborative effort with the housewife and her friends. One of the

TAHINI AND PARSLEY SAUCE
(BAKDONSYEH)

1 clove garlic
2 tbl tahini
½ cup water
½ cup lemon juice
1 cup chopped parsley
1 tsp cumin

1. Mash the garlic in a mixing bowl, then blend in the tahini. Gradually add water and lemon juice, and continue blending until the sauce becomes smooth. Fold in the chopped parsley, season with cumin, and serve.

2. This sauce is usually served as an appetizer dip for pita bread or with fried fish. It also could be served as a dip with fresh vegetables.

Yields 8 servings

Nutrient value per serving:

Calories   30
Fat   2 grams
Cholesterol   0
Fiber   less then one gram
Sodium   10 milligrams

TANOOR

women rolls out a piece of dough, then passes it to another woman who tosses it on her hands until it reaches the desirable thickness and size, and she in turn passes it to a third woman, who places the loaf on a round cotton pillow. Now comes the delicate part of the operation. Using the pillow on which the flattened dough is placed, this last woman literally tosses the dough onto the hot clay wall inside the tanoor, and, amazingly, the dough sticks to the wall. It takes no more than a couple of minutes to have a finished loaf, which is removed with great speed by the woman tending to the tanoor itself.

CUMIN-YOGURT SAUCE
(KAMMOUN WA LABAN)

1 cup plain nonfat yogurt
½ cup lemon juice
2 tbs cumin
3 cloves garlic, *mashed*

1. Combine all the ingredients and blend to a smooth paste.

Yields 8 servings

Nutrient value per Serving:

Calories	35
Fat	less then one gram
Cholesterol	0
Fiber	0
Sodium	35 milligrams

TAHINI AND POMEGRANATE SAUCE
(TAHINI WA RUMMAN)

2 tbl tahini
¼ cup pomegranate paste
½ cup water
1 tsp cumin
2 cloves garlic
½ tsp red pepper

1. Combine all the ingredients in a food processor and blend to a smooth paste. Adjust the amount of water depending on the degree of thickness you prefer.

2. Serve as a dip for roasted vegetables and chicken.

Yields 8 servings

Nutrient value per serving:

Calories	65
Fat	2 grams
Cholesterol	0
Fiber	less then one gram
Sodium	10 milligrams

SPICY WALNUT SAUCE
(SALSIT JUOZ HAR)

If you can't find the *harisa* in a store, substitute a sweet red bell pepper mixed with 1 tsp of red chili pepper, puréed into a paste in a blender.

1 medium onion, *finely chopped*
4-5 cloves garlic
½ cup walnuts, *mashed*
½ cup lemon juice
½ cup water
3 tbl *harisa*
1 tbl olive oil
1 tbl cumin
1 tbl ground coriander
1 tbs paprika

1. Over low heat, sauté the chopped onions until transparent. Add the garlic and walnuts, and sauté for 5 minutes. Remove from the heat and add the rest of the ingredients, mixing well. Put the mixture back on the stove and cook for 2–3 minutes. This sauce is mainly used on hot fish dishes and with roasted vegetables.

Yields 10 servings

Nutrient value per serving:

Calories	75
Fat	6 grams
Cholesterol	0
Fiber	1 grams
Sodium	10 milligrams

Chapter Seven
Meatless Rice and
Bulgur Dishes

RICE AND EGGPLANT MOLD
(MAKLOBET MSAKAA')

1 large eggplant
1 cup chopped onion
1 tbl olive oil
2 cups diced tomatoes
1 cup rice
1½ cups water
pepper to taste

Nutrient value per serving:

Calories	200
Fat	4 grams
Cholesterol	0
Fiber	8 grams
Sodium	30 milligrams

1. Peel the eggplant and slice into ½-inch thick slices. Place them on a cookie sheet and spray lightly with oil, and then broil until they have turned golden brown. The traditional recipe calls for frying the eggplant, but broiling avoids excess calories, and amazingly, the resulting flavor is much better.

2. Sauté the onions in oil until tender, then add the tomatoes and cook for an additional 5 minutes.

3. Arrange the eggplant in the bottom of a cooking pot. On top of the eggplant, spread half of the onion and tomato mixture, then over that spread the rice, and finally the remainder of the onion and tomatoes. Add the pepper and the water, and cook over low heat for 30 minutes or until the rice is done. Place a serving plate on top of the pot and turn both the pot and the serving dish upside-down, creating a cake in the shape of the cooking pot. Wait 5 minutes; then remove the pan.

Yields 4 servings

BULGUR WHEAT WITH TOMATOES AND ONION
(BURGHUL BEL BANADOURA)

1 cup chopped onions
1 tbl olive oil
4 very ripe tomatoes, or 2 cups of diced canned tomatoes
3 cups water
1 tbl tomato paste
pepper to taste
1 cup #3 bulgur wheat
1 cup cooked chickpeas

1. Sauté the onions in olive oil until translucent. Add the tomatoes and sauté for an additional 5 minutes. Add the water, tomato paste, and the pepper, and allow the mixture to boil, then stir in the bulgur and the beans. Cook for about 25 minutes or until the water evaporates and the bulgur is no longer chewy.

Yields 4 servings

Nutrient value per serving:

Calories   180
Fat   5 grams
Cholesterol   0 grams
Fiber   6.5 grams
Sodium   25 milligrams

BULGUR WHEAT WITH LENTILS
(MOJADDERAH)

1 cup lentils, *washed*
7 cups water
1 cup coarse #3 bulgur
2 cups onions, *sliced into slivers*
1 tbl olive oil
2 tsp cumin

Nutrient value per serving:

Calories	355
Fat	4 grams
Cholesterol	0
Fiber	18 grams
Sodium	25 milligrams

1. Rinse lentils and bring them to a boil in the water. Continue boiling until the lentils are soft. Make sure about 2 cups of water remain after boiling the lentils. If there is not, add enough water to make 2 cups of extra liquid. Add the bulgur and cook over medium heat.

2. While the bulgur is cooking, sauté the onions in the olive oil until crispy brown, in fact, until they're almost burned. You might think this is weird, but cooking the onions this way give this dish its distinctive taste. Remove the onions from the frying pan and set aside.

3. To use all the oil remaining in the frying pan, put a couple of tablespoons of the bulgur and lentil mixture in to soak it up, then return this mixture back into the cooking pot. Continue cooking until the bulgur is soft and the water has evaporated.

4. Place everything on a platter and spread the browned onions on top. This dish is delicious served either hot or cold.

Yields 4 servings

RICE WITH LENTILS
(MDERDARA)

2 onions, *sliced into slivers*
1 tbl olive oil
1 cup lentil
7 cups water
1 tbl cumin
pepper to taste
1 cup rice

1. Sauté the onions in the olive oil until crispy brown. Add the lentils, water, cumin, and the pepper. Bring to a boil. Cook until the lentils are soft. Make sure that you have at least two cups of liquid left before you add the rice. Add the rice and cook over low heat until the water has evaporated and the rice is done.

Yields 4 servings

Nutrient value per serving:

Calories	390
Fat	4 grams
Cholesterol	0
Fiber	12 grams
Sodium	20 milligrams

" Mojadderah," *writes Khalid, "has a marvellous effect upon my humor and nerves... After a good round pewter platter of this delicious dish and a dozen leeks, I feel as if I could do the work of all mankind. And I am then in such a beatific state of mind that I would share with mankind my sack of lentils and my pipkin of olive oil."*
—*from* The Book of Khalid
by Ameen Rihani; 1911.

RICE WITH VERMICELLI NOODLES
(RUZ BEL-SHA'IRIYA)

½ cup vermicelli noodles, *broken into 1-inch lengths*
1 tbl oil
2 cups water, *salted to taste*
1 cup rice

1. Brown the vermicelli noodles in the oil. Add water and salt to taste, and allow the mixture to boil. Add the rice. Cook for 10 minutes over medium heat, and then simmer for 15 minutes on very low heat. Rice cooked this way is served as a side dish with most stews.

Yields 4 servings

Nutrient value per serving:

Calories 220
Fat 4 grams
Cholesterol 0
Fiber 0.7 gram
Sodium 20 milligrams

RICE WITH TOMATO
(RUZ WA BANADOURA)

1 small onion, *chopped*
1 tbl olive oil
1 small ripe tomato, *diced*
2 cups water
1 tbl tomato paste
½ tsp black pepper
1 cup rice

1. Sauté the onion in the olive oil until transparent. Add the diced tomato and cook for couple of minutes. Add the water, tomato paste, and the pepper. Bring to a boil, then add the rice. Cover and simmer over low heat for 20 minutes or until rice is tender and the juice has been absorbed.

Yields 4 servings

Nutrient value per serving:

Calories 260
Fat 4 grams
Cholesterol 0
Fiber 2 grams
Sodium 30 milligrams

Clockwise from top: Stuffed Grape Leaves (page 144), Eggplant Spread with Tahini (page 35),
Pickled Cucumbers, Red Pepper Spread (page 46), Pickled Turnips, Eggplant Spread (page 36),
with Hummus (page 33) in the middle.

*Stuffed Zucchini and Stuffed Eggplant with tomato sauce (pages 42-43),
with Sautéed Spinach (page 121).*

Potato Salad (page 52), Cucumber and Radish Salad (page 58), and Chickpea Salad (page 55).

Clockwise from top left: Split Pea Soup (page 71), Lentil Lemon Soup (page 64), and Lentil Cream Soup (page 68).

*Clockwise from top left: Swiss Chard with Bulgur (page 92), Bulgur Wheat with Lentils (page 166),
and Bulgur Wheat with Tomatoes and Onion (page 83).*

Clockwise from top left: Rice with Vermicelli Noodles (page 86), Mixed Salad (page 53), and Rice with Carrots and Peas (page 89).

Clockwise from top: Cheese Balls (page 100), Bulgur and Yogurt Spread (page 33), and Yogurt Cream Cheese (page 98).

*Clockwise from top left: Green Fava Beans with Cilantro (page 110),
Green Bean Stew (page 120), and Eggplant Stew (page 111).*

Clockwise from top left: Sautéed Spinach (page 121), Cauliflower in Tomato Sauce (page 118), and Artichoke Bottoms Stuffed with Herbs (page 124).

Thin Steak in Garlic Lemon Sauce (page 140), with Roasted Potatoes (page 132).

Large Salmon with Spicy Walnut Sauce (page 166).

Milk and Orange Pudding (page 172), and Arabic Coffee with Cardamom.

RICE WITH ORANGE LENTILS AND RAISINS

(RUZ BEL ADAS WA ZABEEB)

4 cups water
1 cup orange lentils
1 small onion,
finely chopped
1 tbl olive oil
½ cup red bell pepper,
chopped
¼ cup green bell pepper,
chopped
½ cup raisins
1 tbl chopped
fresh ginger
2 whole cloves
1 tsp allspice
½ tsp black pepper
¼ tsp saffron, *optional*
1 cup rice

1. Boil the lentils in water until soft but firm. Drain the lentils and set aside, saving 2½ cups of the water. If you don't have enough water, just add more.

2. In a heavy pot sauté the onion until transparent; then add the red and green peppers, raisins, ginger, cloves, and allspice. Stir and sauté for 2 minutes. Add the water and bring to boil. Add the rice, stir and cook over low heat until the water is absorbed. Stir in the lentils and serve.

Yields 6 servings

Nutrient value per serving:

Calories	290
Fat	3 grams
Cholesterol	0
Fiber	9 grams
Sodium	15 milligrams

BULGUR AND BLACK-EYED PEAS
(BURGHUL WA LOBEYEH HAB)

1 tbl olive oil

1 small onion, *chopped*

2 cloves garlic, *mashed*

2 cups black-eyed peas, *frozen*

3 cups water

1 cup # 3 bulgur

½ cup chopped cilantro

pepper to taste

1. Sauté the onion and garlic in the olive oil. Thaw the black-eyed peas, add and cook over low heat for 5 minutes, stirring occasionally and adding a couple of spoons of water to prevent sticking.

2. Pour in the remaining water and bring it to boil. Add the bulgur, cilantro and pepper and cook over low heat until the water has evaporated and the bulgur is no longer chewy.

Yields 4 servings

Nutrient value per serving:

Calories	280
Fat	4 grams
Cholesterol	0
Fiber	14 grams
Sodium	15 milligrams

RICE WITH CARROTS AND PEAS
(RUZ WA JAZAR WA BAZELEH)

1 small onion, *chopped*
1 tbl olive oil
1 cup carrots,
cut into ½-inch cubes
1 cup sweet peas
2½ cups water
1 tbl allspice
pepper to taste
1 cup rice

1. Sauté the onion in the olive oil until transparent. Add the rest of the vegetables and sauté, over low heat, for 5 minutes. Add the water and the seasoning and bring to boil. Add the rice and cook over low heat until the water has evaporated and the rice is done.

Yields 4 servings

Nutrient value per serving:

Calories	255
Fat	4 grams
Cholesterol	0
Fiber	3.8 grams
Sodium	15 milligrams

BULGUR AND VERMICELLI NOODLES
(RUZ BEL SHA'IRIYA)

1 cup vermicelli noodles
1 tbl olive oil
2½ cups water
¼ tbl black pepper
1 cup #3 bulgur

1. Sauté the vermicelli noodles in the olive oil until light brown. Add the water and the pepper. Bring the water to boil; then add the bulgur and simmer over low heat until the water has been absorbed.

Yields 4 servings

Nutrient value per serving:

Calories 200
Fat 4 grams
Cholesterol 0
Fiber 7 grams
Sodium 40 milligrams

عِنْدَ ٱلْبُطُونِ ضَاعَتِ ٱلْعُقُولُ

"Busy stomachs, absent minds."

BULGUR AND POTATO BURGER WITH MUSHROOM STUFFING
(KEBBET BATATA)

1 large potato

1 cup # 1 bulgur

2 large onions,

½ for the dough and

1½ for the filling

1 cup whole wheat flour

½ tsp red pepper

2 tbls olive oil

2 cups sliced mushrooms

1 tsp allspice

pepper to taste

Nutrient value per serving:

Calories	180
Fat	4 grams
Cholesterol	0
Fiber	6 grams
Sodium	15 milligrams

1. Boil the potato until done. Remove the skin and cut it into four parts. Wash the bulgur and let it sit in a cup of water until the bulgur is soft. In the food processor, put the potato, bulgur, and half an onion, and purée until you have a very sticky dough. Put this sticky potato dough in a mixing bowl. Add the flour and red pepper and mix thoroughly. Add more flour if the dough remains very sticky.

2. Chop the remaining onions. In a heavy pot and over low heat, sauté them in 1 tablespoon of olive oil until transparent. Add the mushrooms and allspice and cook for 5 minutes.

3. Spray a 9 x 12 x 3-inch baking dish with olive oil spray. Spread one half of the dough on the bottom of the dish, patting evenly with your wet hand. Spread the mushroom and onion stuffing over the dough layer. Divide the other half of the dough into several balls and form small patties from them. Lay them over the top of the filling. Patch them over the filling, making sure to wet your hand with water to prevent sticking. Pour 1 tablespoon of olive oil in your hand and rub your palms together, then smooth the top of the dough.

4. Bake in a 375° oven for 10 minutes. Remove the dish from the oven and cut the burger into 3-inch squares. Return to the oven and bake for 40–50 minutes, or until cooked through.

Yields 8 servings

SWISS CHARD WITH BULGUR
(SELEK WA BURGHUL)

1 medium onion, *chopped*
3 garlic cloves, *mashed*
1 tbl olive oil
1 lb Swiss chard,
chopped into small pieces
½ cup #3 bulgur wheat
1 cup water
pepper to taste

Nutrient value per serving:

Calories	130
Fat	4 grams
Cholesterol	0
Fiber	5.7 grams
Sodium	250 milligrams

1. Sauté the onion and garlic in the olive oil until the onion is transparent. Add the Swiss chard to the onion and garlic and let them cook, over medium heat, between 6 to 10 minutes or until the Swiss chard has reduced in bulk. Make a hole in the center of the Swiss chard, add the bulgur, then cover it with the chard. Cook for 5 more minutes. Season with pepper. Add water and cook over low heat until the water has evaporated.

Yields 4 servings

BULGUR WITH PARSLEY AND TOMATO
(BURGHUL WA BAKDOONES)

3 medium tomatoes
2 cups parsley
1 medium onion
1 red bell pepper
1 tbl olive oil
1 cup #1 bulgur
1 tsp cumin
¼ tsp ground coriander
1½ cups water
2 tbl pomegranate molasses

1. Put the tomatoes, parsley, onion and the red pepper in a food processor and purée them. Sauté the puréed vegetables in the olive oil for a couple of minutes. Add the bulgur, coriander, and cumin, then cook for another couple of minutes. Pour in the water and the pomegranate molasses. Cook over low heat until the bulgur is soft and the water has evaporated.

Yields 6 servings

Nutrient value per serving:

Calories 225
Fat 5 grams
Cholesterol 0
Fiber 9 grams
Sodium 40 milligrams

Chapter Eight
Dairy

One of my fondest childhood memories is of spending the night at my grandparents' home in the village. We lived in Damascus until June, when school was over for the year. My father then routinely sent us to the village for the summer. My brothers and sister were small, so after my mother fed us dinner she would have us put on our pajamas. We would then walk over to our grandparents' home. That was when the story-telling ritual would start. Our grandmother would tell us the tales we loved to hear—but only if we promised her that we had been good to our mother that day. After sworn testimony that we had behaved, she would tell us a story. This was before we had television, when hearing a story was one of the greatest moments of our lives. Fortunately, the stories were different every night, ranging from Ala'adin and Sinbad to animal stories. Inevitably, the story was so long that there was only time for one story a night.

Early in the morning, we were usually awakened by the sound of my grandmother's voice outside our bedroom. She was sitting on a thin mattress on the ground making butter. She held a *khabeh*, a large clay pot, between her legs, shaking the cream inside, changing it into butter.

My grandfather would sit next to her drinking *mete*, a drink that originated in South America, and was brought back to the Middle East by Syrian immigrants returning home.

As my grandmother shook the *khabeh*, small particles of butter would form on the cover. This was her signal to pour the entire contents into a wide shallow container. After about thirty minutes the butter would come to the surface. She would skim it off with her hands and form it into a ball. From this she would make *ghee*, clarified butter. The white liquid that remains after the butter has formed is a sort of buttermilk or non-fat yogurt called *ayraan*. It has a wonderful flavor, and I loved to drink it. My grandmother would sell the butter and boil the *ayraan*, making a kind of cottage cheese.

It goes without saying that I grew up eating and learning to love the variety of homemade cheeses that came from my grandmother's kitchen.

YOGURT
(LABAN)

1 quart skim milk
¼ cup plain non-fat
yogurt for starter

Nutrient value per serving:

Calories 95
Fat less then one gram
Cholesterol 5 mg
Fiber 0
Sodium 140 milligrams

1. Bring the milk to a boil. Immediately remove from the heat and cool to 120°. Test by immersing your little finger and counting to 10. Thin the starter with some of the warm milk in a separate bowl, and then mix with the rest of the milk.

2. Cover the pot and wrap well with a blanket and let stand for 7-8 hours or overnight. Refrigerate for a couple hours before using.

Yields 4 servings

NEW YEAR'S DAY

Damascus residents have a tradition of cooking what is called a "white dish" on New Year's Day to insure that the new year will be a "white," or lucky, year. Anything white suffices to fulfill this superstition, such as yogurt, or a milk dish.

YOGURT DRINK
(AYRAAN)

3 cups non-fat yogurt
1 cup water
1 clove of garlic, *optional*

1. Beat all the ingredients well in a bowl or the blender. Chill and serve.

Yields 4 cups

Nutrient value per serving:
Calories   100
Fat   less then one gram
Cholesterol   4 milligrams
Fiber   less then one gram
Sodium   150 milligrams

YOGURT CREAM CHEESE
(LABNEH)

4 cups Yogurt
(see page 97)

1. Stir the yogurt and pour into a cheesecloth bag. Hang the bag for about 10 hours, until all the liquid has drained. What remains is a thick creamy spread, similar to cream cheese, but not sweet. Cover and refrigerate the cheese.

2. To serve, place in a shallow dish with a touch of olive oil.

Nutrient value per serving:
Calories   130
Fat   less then one gram
Cholesterol   5 milligrams
Fiber   0
Sodium   195 milligrams

Yields 4 servings

YOGURT SOUP
(LABAN MATBOKH)

This yogurt soup is used in several recipes.

1 cup water
½ cup cornstarch
5 cups non-fat plain yogurt
½ cup rice
4 cloves garlic, *mashed*
1 tbl dry mint

Nutrient value per serving:

Calories	155
Fat	less then one gram
Cholesterol	5 milligrams
Fiber	0
Sodium	165 milligrams

1. Mix the water and cornstarch. Place the yogurt, cornstarch paste and the rice in a heavy saucepan. Mix well and cook over medium heat, stirring constantly in one direction with a wooden spoon, being careful not to scorch it. Bring to a boil; add the mashed garlic and the dry mint. Turn down the heat and cook for 15-20 minutes or until the yogurt is thick and soup-like. Serve hot or cold.

Yields 8 servings

CHEESE BALLS
(LABNEH MAKBOSEH)

4 cups Yogurt Cream
Cheese, (see page 98)
1 tsp red pepper, *optional*
1 tbl nigella, or poppy seeds,
optional

Nutrient value per ball:

Calories   160
Fat   less then one gram
Cholesterol   6 milligrams
Fiber   0
Sodium   235 milligrams

1. Mix all the ingredients together. Make walnut size balls, using a little oil on the palm of your hands to prevent sticking. Place the balls on a towel for 8 hours to drain away the extra moisture.

2. Pack the balls into sterilized jars and refrigerate. To serve, place three or more balls in a dish with some olive oil. They are ready to spread on bread, toast or bagels.

Yields 10 balls

جوِّع كَلبَك يَتبَعك

"Keep your dog hungry, and it will follow you."

BASIC CHEESE
(JEBNEH BYDAH)

I gallon skim milk
4 junket rennet tablets
2 tbs water
I tbl nigella or poppy
seeds, *optional*

Nutrient value per piece:

Calories	140
Fat	I gram
Cholesterol	8 milligrams
Fiber	0
Sodium	210 milligrams

1. Heat the milk to lukewarm. Crush the junket rennet tablets in a cup and dissolve in the water. Add the mixture to the milk, and stir well. Cover and set aside for I hour to become firm.

2. Stir the firm milk to break the curds. If you are going to add the nigella seeds, do so now. Cover a large strainer with cheesecloth, place it over a bowl, and strain the curds, collecting the whey in the bowl. The whey should be saved for use in other recipes, such as the Boiled Cheese (*halloumi*).

3. Place a cloth—I use an old pillowcase—over a board. Move the drained curds to the board and shape them, with the help of the cloth, into squares 2-inches thick. Press down on the cloth to drain out all the remaining liquid. You have just made basic cheese.

4. If the cheese is to be served fresh or used for dessert, do not add salt. Otherwise, to preserve, cut the cheese into 2-inch cubes, sprinkle them with about 2 tablespoons of pickling salt and refrigerate overnight. The next day, boil 2 quarts of water and ½ cup pickling salt, then leave to cool. Put the cheese in a sterilized jar and cover it with the cold salt water. Cheese stored this way keeps for several months.

Yields 10 pieces
(approximately 2 ounces each)

BOILED CHEESE
(HALLOUMI)

Halloumi tastes best when sliced and fried—without oil or butter—then eaten in a sandwich, with a slice of onion if you like. It is similar to *scamorze*, an Italian cheese that is either grilled or broiled to bring out its wonderful flavor.

I recipe of Basic Cheese, including the leftover (see page 101)

Nutrient value per piece:

Calories	260
Fat	I gram
Cholesterol	10 milligrams
Fiber	0
Sodium	600 milligrams

I. In a pot, bring the whey to a boil. Cut the cheese into 2-inch cubes, and drop into the boiling whey. Cook until the cheese floats. Remove the cheese and set aside. The cheese may be eaten fresh or refrigerated to store.

Yields 10 pieces

SPICED CHEESE
(SHANKLEESH)

8 oz fat-free cottage cheese
1 cup Yogurt Cream Cheese,
(see page 98)
1 tbl garlic powder
1 tsp red pepper
1 tsp black pepper
¼ cup thyme

Nutrient value per ball:

Calories 320
Fat 1 gram
Cholesterol 20 milligrams
Fiber 1 gram
Sodium 700 milligrams

1. The cottage cheese should be drained for at least 24 hours to make a good spiced cheese.

2. Mix the cottage cheese and the Yogurt Cream Cheese together. Add the garlic powder and peppers to the cheese, and knead until the spices are mixed well. Taste the cheese and adjust the spices to your taste.

3. Roll the cheese into balls 2 inches in diameter. Place on a cloth in a dry area for 24 hours. Dip and roll the balls in the thyme until they are completely covered. This cheese can be eaten plain, or in an omelet, or with olive oil, chopped onion and chopped tomato, which makes a tasty spiced cheese salad.

Yields 2 balls

AGED SPICED CHEESE
(SHANKLEESH)

After making spiced cheese, place the cheese balls into an airtight jar for 15 to 20 days. The longer you age it the stronger it gets, so the amount of aging depends on your taste. When you want to eat it, remove the balls from the jar and wash the mold that will have formed around them. Roll the balls in thyme, put into a jar and refrigerate.

Chapter Nine
Vegetable Dishes

Most Levantine side dishes are meatless, making them superbly healthy main courses for those who eat no meat, and who want a low-fat and high-fiber diet. What is special about dishes that contain a mix of beans and grain (for example, beans and rice, bulgur wheat and chickpeas, pasta and beans) is that these mixtures supply our bodies with a complete protein, making eating animal products completely unnecessary. In most Arab countries these dishes are generally thought of as "peasant food," but you will notice, when a restaurant or a deli in the West advertises "healthy food," generally Levantine dishes such as *tabbouli* and *hummus* are in the forefront. Middle East "peasants" to this day derive most of their protein from these dishes.

My husband tells me that when he was growing up in rural South Dakota, a state where meat and potatoes were, and still are, the staple with most families, he noticed that his mother cooked and served highly unusual dishes. She cooked rice wrapped in grape leaves, picked every fall along the creek bottoms south of their village of Wood, or she hollowed out zucchini squash and stuffed them with a rice mixture. He asked her why their food tasted so much better than the food eaten by most other people in their town. She told him that in south Lebanon, where she grew up in the late 1800s and early 1900s, there was no money to buy food, so it all had to come from their own gardens or from the wild. "It was all we had," she told him.

There is something to be said for the fact that long before nutritional science taught us that beans and grain mixed together provide us with complete protein, or before we learned that high-fiber meals cut the risk of cancer and heart disease, Arab women have always been aware of the health benefits of such cooking.

Recently, when I visited my family in our village in Syria, I tried to explain to my 90-year old grandmother how healthy and well-balanced her cooking was. At that time she still took care of her own home and her 96-year old husband, but she snapped at me that she had no idea what I was talking about. She calls me a part of the "powdered-milk generation," because we didn't nurse at our mother's breast, which, she claims, is why the world is deteriorating, and none of us will ever come to any good.

↓

Fava beans have been, and still are, the major source of protein for low-income families in a number of Arab countries. In Egypt, as well as in the old section of Damascus, a pushcart stove, called an *arabaya*, is a familiar sight. The bed of the cart has a large hole in its center; in there, a fire heats a copper pot of continuously cooking fava beans. Like the Good Humor man here in America, the fava bean vendor rolls through the neighborhoods, singing out his song announcing his wares. Housewives send their children out with a pan and money enough to buy what they need for the morning. The fava bean vendor always seemed to be familiar, almost intimate, with each family, asking the children how their parents were faring, whether or not anyone was sick, and in general keeping up with neighborhood gossip.

Arab children not only are a help to their mothers when they buy fava beans from the vendor, but they learn a valuable lesson in bargaining, a wonderful part of the culture of the Arab World. When the pan is filled by the vendor, the child will usually ask for another helping. When the vendor refuses, the child will argue that his neighbor received more with the same money, and on and on until one or the other gives up.

Bargaining is part of everyone's life in the Arab world. Most Westerners, I've found, are too bashful to bargain, just because it's not typical of their culture. They have missed a lot.

There are millions of bargaining stories, but one of my favorites is told by my husband. He and his older brother, Chick, were in Cairo in the 1970s, and Chick wanted to buy a carved copper tray to take home. My husband took him to a shop in the *souk* where he found the one he wanted. "How much for that tray?" my husband asked.

"Eight Egyptian pounds," the shopkeeper said in surprisingly good English.

"I'll give you five pounds for it," my husband replied.

The merchant's hand went to his heart, looking at the moment very much like the American comedian, Redd Foxx.

"Five pounds? Five pounds? What do you expect from us? Five pounds? We are poor people. You cannot get blood from a stone." He raged on, pouring on guilt and anything else he could think of, to my husband's everlasting enjoyment.

"I'll tell you what I'll do," he said after he wound down. "I'll take six pounds for it."

My husband, who by then was doubled up with laughter, gave him seven pounds— "One extra for the show," he told the merchant.

And Danny Thomas used to tell this story about a trip he took to Lebanon. He was in a hurry to get to the airport to return to the United States when he remembered he hadn't bought a gift for his wife. He stopped at a small shop in Beirut and asked the merchant how much he wanted for a set of china coffee cups that were displayed in the shop.

"Ten Lebanese pounds," the merchant replied.

"Wrap them up, I'll take them," Thomas told him, visibly nervous about catching his plane.

"Wait just a minute," the merchant said, almost in shock. "Did I say something wrong? Why don't you sit down and have some coffee and we'll discuss this," he told an increasingly panicked Thomas. He was upset because Thomas had accepted his first price. The vendor had obviously fully expected to spend a few minutes bargaining.

One other bargaining technique is often used. A number of years ago, my husband and Senator Thomas Eagleton were in the Hamadieh Souk in Damascus looking for bargains. My husband found a small bag he wanted to buy, and began bargaining with the shopkeeper. When my husband refused to give in to the shopkeeper's last price, the shopkeeper shouted, "Here. If you're such a *mokhtar* (a village leader), then take it free." My husband, embarrassed, (which was, of course, the shopkeeper's intention) paid the last price offered, much to the delight of Senator Eagleton.

But as often as this technique has been used, I know of no-one who has ever called the merchant's bluff. I imagine if someone were to take the item without paying, the shopkeeper would call the police. But it is true that in the Arab world if a buyer doesn't bargain, the merchant loses respect for him.

Now, some of the best bargains in the Arab world: delicious meatless dishes.

> *"Do not make your stomach*
> *a grave for animals."*
> —*Khalifa Ali*

FAVA BEANS
(FUL MUDAMMAS)

1 clove garlic
½ cup lemon juice
1 medium tomato, *diced*
1 small chopped onion
½ cup finely chopped parsley
1 tbl olive oil
1 tbl ground cumin
pepper to taste
2½ cups cooked fava beans

1. Mash (or press) the garlic, mix it with the lemon juice and add it and the remainder of the ingredients to the beans. You can, if you want, mix the lemon juice, olive oil, and the seasoning in with the beans, leaving the vegetables in separate bowls. *Ful* is eaten with bread and raw onions. Stuffed into a small pita, it makes a delightful sandwich.

Yields 4 servings

Nutrient value per serving:

Calories	185
Fat	4 grams
Cholesterol	0
Fiber	7 grams
Sodium	15 milligrams

GREEN FAVA BEANS WITH CILANTRO
(FUL BEL ZEYT)

1 cup chopped onion
3 cloves of minced garlic
1 tbl olive oil
4 cups of fresh, green fava beans (*ful akhdar*)
1 cup chopped cilantro
pepper to taste

Nutrient value per serving:

Calories	240
Fat	4 grams
Cholesterol	0
Fiber	10 grams
Sodium	15 milligrams

1. Sauté the onion in the oil until it is lightly browned. Add the beans and cook over low heat for 20 minutes. Add water if necessary to prevent sticking.

2. Toss the chopped cilantro, minced garlic and the pepper with the beans and cook for 5 additional minutes.

Yields 4 servings

EGGPLANT STEW
(MNAZALIT BATINJAN)

1 large eggplant,
sliced ½-inch thick
2 large onions, *sliced*
1 tbl olive oil
1 cup cooked chickpeas
pepper to taste
1 cup water

Nutrient value per serving:

Calories	170
Fat	5 grams
Cholesterol	0
Fiber	7 grams
Sodium	15 milligrams

1. Place the eggplant slices on a cookie sheet, spray them with olive oil spray and broil them until golden brown.

2. Sauté the onions in olive oil until they are translucent—about 3 minutes. Divide the onions in half, leaving one part in the pan and setting the other temporarily aside.

3. Add half the broiled eggplant, then half the tomatoes, to the onions in the pan and put all chickpeas on the top. Repeat by layering the rest of the onions, the eggplant then the tomatoes on top. Now add the pepper and the water and cook for 20 minutes over medium heat.

Yields 4 servings

ZUCCHINI WITH BULGUR WHEAT
(KOOSA BEL BURGHUL)

1 cup chopped onions
1 tbl olive oil
2 zucchini
1 clove garlic
¼ cup chopped cilantro
1½ cup water
1 cup #3 bulgur
pepper to taste

1. Sauté the onions in the oil until tender. Cut the zucchini into 1-inch cubes and add to the onions, along with the garlic and cilantro. Cook for about 10 minutes, adding a couple of tbs of water to prevent sticking. Add the water. When it comes to a boil, add the bulgur and the pepper and cook for 15-20 minutes, stirring occasionally.

Yields 4 servings

Nutrient value per serving:

Calories	180
Fat	4 grams
Cholesterol	0
Fiber	8 grams
Sodium	15 milligrams

ZUCCHINI IN TAHINI SAUCE
(KOOSA BEL TAHINI)

4 medium zucchini,
sliced into ½-inch rounds
2 cups sliced mushrooms
1 cup chopped onions
1 tbl olive oil
½ tsp allspice
1 cup Tahini and Parsley
Sauce, (see page 77)

Nutrient value per serving:

Calories	120
Fat	6 grams
Cholesterol	0
Fiber	4.5 grams
Sodium	20 milligrams

1. Place the zucchini rounds on a cookie sheet and spray them with olive oil spray. Broil until the edges are golden brown. The original recipe calls for frying, but broiling eliminates both extra calories and a big mess.

2. Line the bottom of the oven dish with zucchini rounds and sliced mushrooms. Spread on the chopped onion and sprinkle with allspice, then pour the Tahini and Parsley Sauce on top. Cover with aluminum foil and bake at 350° for 15 minutes.

Yields 4 servings

ZUCCHINI AND POTATO WITH TOMATOES
(KWAJ)

1 large potato
1 large onion, *chopped*
2 tbs olive oil
4 zucchini squash,
cut into 1-inch cubes
1 eggplant,
cut into 1-inch cubes
1 cup cooked chickpeas
6 large ripe tomatoes,
finely diced
pepper to taste
2 cups water
2 tbs tomato paste
4 basil leaves, *torn*

1. Boil the potatoes until they are half soft. Remove the skin and cut them into 1-inch cubes.

2. Sauté the onions in the oil until transparent. Add the zucchini and eggplant; then cook over medium heat for 10 minutes. Add the chickpeas, the diced tomatoes and the pepper and cook for 5 minutes.

3. Mix the water with the tomato paste, and pour over the zucchini. Add the potatoes and the basil to the pot and simmer for 15 minutes.

Yields 6 servings

Nutrient value per serving:

Calories 140
Fat 4 grams
Cholesterol 0
Fiber 6.5 grams
Sodium 35 milligrams

ZUCCHINI WITH MINT
(KOOSA BEL NA'ANA'A)

4 zucchini
1 cup chopped onion
1 tbl olive oil
2 tbs mint,
dry or fresh
pepper to taste

1. Cut the zucchini into 1-inch cubes. Sauté the onions in the olive oil until they are golden brown. Add the zucchini, mint, and the pepper. Cook over medium heat for 20 minutes. Sprinkle with water to prevent sticking if necessary.

Nutrient value per serving:

Calories	80
Fat	4 grams
Cholesterol	0
Fiber	3.4 grams
Sodium	10 milligrams

Yields 4 servings

THE ROAD BACK HOME

Usually, when a woman marries, she moves to the home of her husband's family, and when the man marries, his parents usually build another room or two for the new family. Although regrettably it is no longer a practice in my village of Safsafi, Syria, (although some remote villages still have the custom) when my parents were married nearly four decades ago my mother was required to ride a pure white horse throughout the village. Actually, she rode it from her parents' home to her husband's home, but she went on every street throughout the village using the most indirect route, telling everyone goodbye. She was not actually leaving the village, but the custom showed that she would never be able to find her way back to her parents' home.

BAKED CAULIFLOWER WITH TAHINI
(ZAHRA BEL TAHINI)

2 lbs cauliflower florets
I cup Tahini and Parsley
Sauce, (see page 77)
I cup Cumin-Yogurt
Sauce, (see page 78)

Nutrient value per serving:

Calories	145
Fat	7 grams
Cholesterol	0
Fiber	7 grams
Sodium	85 milligrams

I. Bring 4 quarts of water to boil. Drop the cauliflower florets in the boiling water and cook for 3 minutes. This prevents the florets from absorbing a lot of oil and saves cooking time.

2. Drain the florets and then place them on a cookie sheet and spray them with olive oil spray. Broil until the edges are golden brown.

3. Line the bottom of the oven dish with the florets. Mix together ½ cup of boiling water, the Tahini and Parsley Sauce and the Cumin-Yogurt Sauce. Pour this mixture on top the florets. Bake at 350° for 15 minutes.

Yields 4 servings

CAULIFLOWER WITH CILANTRO
(QARNABIT MA'A KUZBARA)

2 lbs cauliflower florets
2 cups cilantro, *chopped*
4 cloves garlic, *mashed*
1 tbl olive oil
2 tbs lemon juice
2 cups water
pepper to taste

Nutrient value per serving:

Calories	100
Fat	4 grams
Cholesterol	0
Fiber	6 grams
Sodium	75 milligrams

1. Bring 2 quarts of water to a boil and drop in the cauliflower florets. Cook for 5 minutes, then remove and drain. Place the florets on a cookie sheet, spray with olive oil spray and broil until golden brown.

2. Sauté the cilantro, garlic and pepper in olive oil for a couple of minutes. Add the broiled cauliflower, lemon juice and water and cook over medium heat for 5 minutes.

Yields 4 servings

CAULIFLOWER IN TOMATO SAUCE
(ZAHRA BEL BANADOURA)

1 head cauliflower
1 large potato
1 large onion
1 clove garlic
1 tbl olive oil
⅓ cup tomato paste
4 cups water
½ tsp dry mint
1 cup boiled chickpeas
pepper to taste

Nutrient value per serving:

Calories	200
Fat	5 grams
Cholesterol	0
Fiber	7.5 grams
Sodium	110 milligrams

1. Break the cauliflower into separate florets. Cut the potato into 1-inch cubes. Chop the onion and mash the garlic.

2. Over low heat, sauté the onions in the oil until transparent. Add the potato, cauliflower and the garlic; then sauté for a couple more minutes. Mix the tomato paste with water, pour over the vegetables and cook for 15 minutes. Add the garbanzo beans, mint and the pepper. Cook for 10 minutes or until the vegetables are tender.

Yields 4 servings

OKRA WITH TOMATOES
(BAMIYAH BEL BANADOURA)

1 lb small okra
1 cup chopped onions
8 cloves garlic, *chopped*
1 cup chopped cilantro
1 tbl olive oil
6 large ripe tomatoes, *diced*
(or 1 16-oz can tomatoes)
1 cup water
pepper to taste

Nutrient value per serving:

Calories	140
Fat	4 grams
Cholesterol	0
Fiber	6 grams
Sodium	35 milligrams

1. Cut off the stems, wash the okra and allow them to completely dry. Place them on a cookie sheet and spray them with olive oil spray. Broil for 5 minutes. This prevents the okra from becoming slimy.

2. Sauté the chopped onions, garlic and cilantro in olive oil. Add the tomatoes and the water and bring the mixture to a boil. Add the okra and pepper and cook over low heat for about 15 minutes. Like most dishes with tomato-based sauces, this is usually served with rice.

Yields 4 servings

ماحدّ بِقُول عَن زَيْتَه عَكِرْ

"No one describes his (olive) oil as crude."

GREEN BEAN STEW
(FASOLYEH BEL ZEYT)

1 lb fresh green beans,
(or 20-oz frozen)
1 cup chopped onions
1 tbl olive oil
2 cloves garlic,
mashed or pressed
1 cup chopped cilantro
pepper to taste

Nutrient value per serving:

Calories	100
Fat	4 grams
Cholesterol	0
Fiber	4.5 grams
Sodium	10 milligrams

1. If you use fresh beans, trim by snipping the ends and removing the strings, then wash and cut them into 2-inch lengths. If using frozen beans, defrost them.

2. Sauté the chopped onions in the oil for a few minutes. Add the beans to that mixture, tossing lightly. If the beans stick to the pan and burn, sprinkle occasionally with water. You will need almost one cup of water. Cook 20-25 minutes until the beans are done. Add the garlic and cilantro, toss, season with pepper and cook for 5 minutes.

Yields 4 servings

SAUTÉED SPINACH
(SABANEKH MKALAYEH)

This method can be used to cook other greens such as dandelions and kale.

6 cups water
4 bunches fresh spinach, *chopped*
1 cup onions, *chopped*
1 tbl olive oil
½ cup cilantro
½ tsp black pepper

1. Bring the water to a boil. Drop in the spinach and cook for 3 minutes. Drain the spinach, let it cool, then squeeze out excess water.

2. Sauté the onions in the oil until golden brown. Add the spinach, cilantro and black pepper and cook for 10 minutes.

Yields 4 servings

Nutrient value per serving:

Calories	100
Fat	4 grams
Cholesterol	0
Fiber	7 grams
Sodium	180 milligrams

GREEN FAVA BEANS IN YOGURT SOUP
(FUL AKHDAR BEL LABAN)

2 onions, *sliced*

1 tbl olive oil

2 lbs green fava beans, *shelled*

(or frozen lima beans)

4 cloves garlic, *mashed*

3 cups Yogurt Soup, (see page 99)

pepper to taste

1. Over medium heat, brown the onions in the oil. Add the fava beans and cook for 15-20 minutes or until the beans are soft. To prevent the beans from burning or sticking to the bottom of the pan, sprinkle occasionally with water.

2. Add the cooked onions, beans and garlic to the yogurt soup. Season with pepper and cook over low heat for 10 minutes, stirring continuously.

Yields 6 servings

Nutrient value per serving:

Calories	290
Fat	3 grams
Cholesterol	4 milligrams
Fiber	9.5 grams
Sodium	110 milligrams

"The stomach is the home of disease, and abstinence is the start of every remedy. So make abstinence your custom."
—The Prophet Mohammad

FAVA BEANS WITH SWISS CHARD
(FUL AKHDAR WA SELEK)

2 lbs green fava beans, *shelled*
1 lb swiss chard, *chopped*
4 cloves garlic, *mashed*
2 cups chopped cilantro
1 large onion, *chopped*
1 tbl olive oil
pepper to taste

Nutrient value per serving:

Calories	235
Fat	3 grams
Cholesterol	0
Fiber	10 grams
Sodium	175 milligrams

1. Brown the onion in the oil until transparent. Add the beans and cook over medium heat for 15 minutes or until the beans are soft. To prevent the beans from sticking to the bottom of the pan sprinkle occasionally with water. Add the Swiss chard and continue to cook for 10 minutes. Add the garlic, the cilantro and the pepper to the cooking beans. Cook over low heat for 10 minutes.

Yields 6 servings

ARTICHOKE BOTTOMS STUFFED WITH HERBS
(MEHSHI ARDICHOKE)

10 artichokes,
or 10 frozen artichoke
bottoms
1 lemon, *sliced*
2 tomatoes, *finely chopped*
1 cup diced green bell pepper
1 cup diced red bell pepper
1 cup chopped spring onions
1 cup chopped parsley
2 tbs chopped fresh mint
2 tbs chopped fresh thyme
1 tbl olive oil
¼ cup lemon juice

1. Stem the artichokes close to the base. Scoop out the choke and trim the base to form a cup. In a heavy pot, bring the water and lemon slices to a boil. Drop the artichoke bottoms into the boiling water and cook until tender. Drain, then set aside. If you are using frozen artichoke bottoms, defrost and place on the plate.

2. Mix the tomatoes with the peppers and all the herbs. Add the oil and lemon juice, and toss well. Place the artichoke bottoms on a shallow plate and stuff them with the herb mixture.

Yields 5 servings

Nutrient value per serving:

Calories	110
Fat	3 grams
Cholesterol	0
Fiber	6 grams
Sodium	100 milligrams

ARTICHOKE BOTTOMS STUFFED WITH RICE AND VEGETABLES
(MEHSHI ARDICHOKE BEL RUZ WAL KHODRA)

10 artichoke bottoms
2 tbs flour
1 garlic clove, *mashed*
¼ tsp white pepper
1 tbl olive oil
1 cup chopped onion
1 cup peas
1 cup finely diced carrots
1 cup rice
¼ tsp ground nutmeg
¼ tsp ground cloves
1 tsp allspice
½ tsp black pepper

Nutrient value per serving:

Calories	260
Fat	6 grams
Cholesterol	0
Fiber	7.5 grams
Sodium	90 milligrams

1. Prepare the artichoke bottoms according to the previous recipe.

2. Save one cup of the water in which they were cooked for sauce. Blend the flour with this water, making sure there are no lumps. Add the garlic and white pepper and cook the sauce until it thickens.

2. In a separate pan heat the oil and sauté the onion, peas and carrots. Add rice, nutmeg, cloves, allspice and pepper and stir for a few minutes. Add 2 cups of water and bring to a boil. Reduce the heat and simmer for 20 minutes or until the rice is tender and the water has been absorbed.

3. To serve, stuff the artichoke bottoms with 2 tbs of the rice mixture. Mound the rest of the rice in the middle of a flat serving dish and arrange the stuffed artichoke bottoms around it. Pour the sauce on top of the artichokes.

Yields 5 servings

CURLY ENDIVE IN OLIVE OIL
(HINDBEH BEL ZEYT)

2 bunches curly endive, *chopped*

1 large onion, *chopped*

1 tbl olive oil

1 cup chopped cilantro

Nutrient value per serving:

Calories	90
Fat	3 grams
Cholesterol	0
Fiber	6 grams
Sodium	10 milligrams

1. Bring a deep pot of water to a boil. Drop in the chopped endive and let it boil for 5 minutes. Drain in a colander and squeeze out all excess water.

2. Sauté the onions in the oil until golden. Add the endive and cilantro and sauté over low heat, for 10 minutes.

Yields 4 servings

CURLY ENDIVE IN GARLIC AND LEMON SAUCE
(HINDBEH BEL TOOM)

2 bunches curly endive, *chopped*
1 tbl olive oil
½ cup lemon juice
3 cloves garlic, *mashed*

1. Bring a deep pot of water to a boil. Drop in the chopped endive and let it boil for 5 minutes. Drain in a colander and squeeze out excess water. Mix olive oil, lemon juice and garlic. Pour over the endive and toss thoroughly.

Yields 4 servings

Nutrient value per serving:

Calories	75
Fat	4 grams
Cholesterol	0
Fiber	7 grams
Sodium	10 milligrams

DAIMEH

The word daimeh *means "forever," and is used when one finishes a meal or a cup of coffee. It is meant to shower blessings on the host, meaning,* insha' allah, *(God willing), food will always be abundant in your home and you will always remember to offer it to your guest. And may God let you keep what you have now, and hope it multiplies.*

I'm always a little embarrassed when I hear the daimeh *articulated. Of course, such courtesy was ingrained in me by my parents. At the time of the death of a friend's grandmother, I went with a group of other friends to pay our respects to the family. I was warned not to use the word* daimeh *at the wake, but in my absent-minded way, I finished the coffee that was served to us, and sure enough, automatically said* daimeh. *I had told the family "may your condition last forever."*

KIDNEY BEANS IN TOMATO SAUCE
(FASOLYEH BEL BANADOURA)

1 large onion, *sliced*
1 tbl olive oil
3 cups boiled kidney beans,
(or any other bean)
3 cups diced tomatoes
1 tsp cumin
1 tsp black pepper

1. Sauté the onions in the olive oil for a few minutes. Drain the kidney beans and mix with the onion. Sauté for two more minutes. Add the diced tomatoes, cumin and black pepper and cook over medium heat for 10 minutes.

Yields 4 servings

Nutrient value per serving:
Calories 250
Fat 5 grams
Cholesterol 0
Fiber 12 grams
Sodium 20 milligrams

THE STORY

Among our folk tales, Asha'ab is a most famous character. He is well known for his obsession with food, and, one might ask, "what is wrong with that?" Ordinarily, there would be nothing wrong with it. But Asha'ab's problem was that his obsession was with food belonging to other people. He became famous because of the shrewd and funny ways he escaped his punishment.

Asha'ab, it is told, heard of big dinner a khalifa ("caliph," or successor to the Prophet Mohammad) was holding in honor of a delegation from another country. As usual, Asha'ab crashed the dinner, eating from every dish on the table, then rushing to the dessert table before anyone

SWISS CHARD LEAVES IN OLIVE OIL
(SELEK BEL ZEYT)

2 lbs Swiss chard, *chopped*
2 medium onions, *chopped*
1 tbl olive oil
2 cloves garlic, *mashed*
2 tbs lemon juice
¼ tsp crushed
red pepper

Nutrient value per serving:

Calories	125
Fat	4 grams
Cholesterol	0
Fiber	5.5 grams
Sodium	480 milligrams

1. Bring a deep pot of water to a boil. Drop the chopped Swiss chard in the boiling water and cook for two minutes. Remove to a colander to drain. Squeeze out excess water from leaves.

2. Brown the onions in the oil. Add garlic and sauté for a couple minutes. Add the chard leaves, lemon juice and pepper. Stir and cook over low heat for 10 minutes.

Yields 4 servings

OF ASHA'AB

else could even finish dinner. The khalifa *saw what Asha'ab was doing, and decided to teach him a lesson. Just when Asha'ab had one piece of a dessert in his mouth and before he had time to chew it, the* khalifa *went to the dessert table and said, "I see someone had a piece of the dessert before our honored guest. This is a disgrace for us." He announced that whoever had done it would be beheaded. Everyone looked at Asha'ab, who had a mouthful of dessert. Without missing a beat, Asha'ab said, "Your honor, I ask that you take care of my wife and children," as he continued eating. Of course everyone laughed and the* khalifa *sent him home with a tray of dessert.*

LENTILS AND DUMPLINGS IN GARLIC LEMON SAUCE
(HURAK BE ESBAOH)

2½ cups lentils
1 large onion, *chopped*
10 cups water
8 clove of garlic, *mashed*
3 cups chopped cilantro
3 tbs olive oil
1 large onion, *sliced*
½ cup lemon juice
3 tbs pomegranate molasses
1 loaf Bread, (see page 28)

Nutrient value per serving:

Calories	345
Fat	6 grams
Cholesterol	0
Fiber	15 grams
Sodium	20 milligrams

1. Wash the lentils and boil them with the chopped onion in the water until soft. Sauté the garlic and cilantro in one tablespoon of olive oil for a couple of minutes. Add the garlic and cilantro mixture, lemon juice, and pomegranate molasses to the lentils. Cook for 10 minutes.

2. By hand, cut the dough into ½-inch balls and drop into the lentils. Cook for another 10 minutes. Pour onto a flat serving dish.

3. Sauté the sliced onion in the rest of the oil until crispy brown. Spread this onion on the top of the lentils for decoration and flavor.

Yields 8 servings

PINTO BEANS IN TOMATO SAUCE
(FASOLYEH BEL BANADOURA)

1 large onion, *sliced*
1 tbl olive oil
2 cups diced tomatoes
2 cups boiled pinto beans
1 large bell pepper, *chopped*
½ tsp red pepper
½ tsp black pepper

1. Sauté the onion in olive oil until transparent. Add the diced tomato and cook for a couple minutes. Add the beans, bell pepper and the seasoning and cook over low heat for 10 minutes.

Yields 4 servings

Nutrient value per serving:

Calories	200
Fat	4 grams
Cholesterol	0
Fiber	10 grams
Sodium	15 milligrams

ROASTED POTATOES
(BATATA BEL FERN)

3 large potatoes
1 cup water
3 tbs lemon juice
1 tbl olive oil
1 tbl garlic powder
1 tbl thyme
1 tbl paprika
½ tsp black pepper
¼ tsp red pepper

1. Boil the potatoes until half cooked—about 10 minutes. Remove the skin and cut them into 1-inch cubes and place them in a baking pan.

2. In a separate bowl whisk the lemon juice, olive oil and water. Add the garlic powder, thyme, paprika, black pepper, and red pepper. Pour this herbal liquid over the potatoes and marinate for an hour. Bake in a 400° oven for about 45 minutes or until golden.

Yields 4 servings

Nutrient value per serving:

Calories	160
Fat	4 grams
Cholesterol	0
Fiber	2.8 milligrams
Sodium	10 milligrams

BAKED POTATOES
(BATATA BEL FERN)

3 large potatoes
2 tbs cornstarch
¾ cup water
¼ cup lemon juice
2 garlic cloves, *mashed*
1 tbl olive oil
1 tbl thyme

Nutrient value per serving:

Calories	160
Fat	4 grams
Cholesterol	0
Fiber	2.5 grams
Sodium	10 milligrams

1. Slice the potatoes into very thin slices. Mix the cornstarch with water, then add the rest of the ingredients and whisk. Spray a small baking pan with olive oil spray. Arrange half of the potatoes in the baking pan, making sure they overlap. Pour about ⅓ of the liquid on top of the potatoes, then arrange the rest of the potatoes on top. Pour on the remaining dressing; making sure you cover all the slices. Bake in a 375° oven for an hour.

Yields 4 servings

Chapter Ten
Main Dishes

A great many Levantine main dishes contain some kind of meat. Although we are now aware that using meat excessively adds calories, fat and cholesterol, our Arab ancestors were able to afford all those extra calories because of the great amounts of exercise they undertook. Walking was a principal means of transportation, and, of course, maintaining their farms required extremely hard physical labor. Eating meat in significant amounts was a rare treat to them, to be afforded only on special occasions, such as harvest time.

Today, most farmers in Syria sell their vegetables in the market early in the morning. Temporarily flushed with money, the farmer will generally stop at a butcher's shop to buy meat, not only because he craves it, but also to show it off to his family when he arrives home.

While most farmers raise chickens, they rarely kill them for food, especially those that are good egg layers. The exception to that rule is when the farmer wants to impress guests who arrive unannounced at mealtime. Driven by centuries of tradition, even the poorest farm family will not allow their guests to go away hungry. That would insult the honor of both guests and hosts.

Tradition dies hard in the Arab world. After the men leave for work in the morning and the children go to school, the women of the family—the grandmother, the married daughters, and the daughters-in law—gather at the parents' home. After they drink coffee they begin cooking for the entire family. In one day I have seen such a group make two to three hundred *kibbeh* rolls, most of them fried, but some grilled and others baked.

While they are cooking the women exchange gossip about their husbands, their children, and, of course, their neighbors. By the time the work is done, everyone knows what is going on in the entire neighborhood. When this happened in our family, my grandfather would walk by the kitchen and shake his head, mumbling something about the BBC originating there.

Back to recipes with meat. If you think I'm trying to discourage you from using meat in your recipes, you're right. You can avoid using meat in every dish and still have the same good taste. Because my husband hasn't eaten meat for twenty-two years, I cook these same recipes without meat, sometimes using mushrooms or potatoes instead. Please use meat sparingly if you want to avoid adding to your cholesterol and fat problems.

THIN STEAKS WITH YOGURT SAUCE
(SHARHAT BEL LABAN WAL FUL)

1 lb sirloin steak, *thinly sliced*

2 medium onions, *sliced*

2 cups young fresh, or frozen, fava beans (or substitute lima beans)

1 tbl olive oil

½ tsp allspice

pepper to taste

1 qt Yogurt Soup (see page 99)

1. Sauté the onions and fava beans in the olive oil until soft. Add water if necessary to prevent sticking. Add the steak and the allspice and pepper and sauté until done. Pour the yogurt sauce on the meat and cook for 15 minutes. Serve this dish with cooked rice mixed with browned angel hair pasta.

Yields 6 servings

Nutrient value per serving:

Calories	285
Fat	6 grams
Cholesterol	50 milligrams
Fiber	4 grams
Sodium	180 milligrams

BEEF FILET WITH YOGURT SOUP
(SHAKREYEH)

1 lb beef filet,
cut into 2-inch chunks
2 cups chopped onion
1 tbl allspice
1 tsp black pepper
1 qt Yogurt Soup,
(see page 99)

1. Cover the beef and the onion with water, add the allspice and pepper and cook for 30 minutes or until the meat is tender. Pour off all liquid except 1 cup of broth. Add the Yogurt Soup. Simmer for 15 minutes, stirring occasionally. Serve this dish with rice.

Yields 6 servings

Nutrient value per serving:

Calories	335
Fat	4 grams
Cholesterol	65 milligrams
Fiber	1 gram
Sodium	315 milligrams

STUFFED ZUCCHINI IN YOGURT SOUP
(SHEIKH AL-MAHSHI)

8 zucchini squash,
up to 6-inches in length
4 oz extra-lean ground beef
1 cup chopped onion
1 tsp cumin
1 tsp allspice
8 cups water
1 qt Yogurt Soup,
(see page 99)
2 cloves garlic, *mashed*

Nutrient value per serving:

Calories	300
Fat	5 grams
Cholesterol	35 milligrams
Fiber	7.5 grams
Sodium	250 milligrams

1. Core the zucchini, leaving ¼-inch walls. Until you gain experience coring, you might pierce a couple, but not to worry. Rinse in cold water and drain by turning them upside down.

2. Sauté the meat in its own fat for a couple minutes. Add the onion, cumin and allspice. Mix well. Stuff the zucchini to the rim with the meat mixture. In a cooking pot bring the eight cups of water to a boil. Drop the zucchini into the boiling water and cook for 10 minutes. Remove the zucchini and save 1 cup of the water.

3. In another cooking pot bring the Yogurt Soup to a boil. Place the zucchini in the soup; then pour in the reserved cooking water and the garlic. Cover and cook over low heat for about 10 minutes.

Yields 4 servings

THIN STEAK IN GARLIC LEMON SAUCE
(SHARHAT MTAFAYEH)

1 lb extra-lean round steak,
thinly sliced
2 tbs allspice
pepper to taste
1 tbl olive oil
10 cloves of garlic, *mashed*
½ cup water
1 cup sliced canned
mushrooms
1 cup sweet peas
(fresh or frozen)
¼ cup lemon juice

Nutrient value per serving:

Calories 300
Fat 10 grams
Cholesterol 105 milligrams
Fiber 2.5 grams
Sodium 235 milligrams

1. If you cannot find thin steaks, buy filet mignon and pound them with a wooden meat tenderizer.

2. Mix the allspice and pepper well. Spread the mixture over the steaks. Heat the olive oil and sauté the steak for a few seconds on each side or until they undergo a slight change of color. Put the steak aside.

3. Sauté the garlic, for a few seconds, in the same pan, after adding a couple tablespoons of water. Add the mushrooms, peas, lemon juice and the rest of the water. Cook for 5 minutes. Return the steaks to the pan; stir into the vegetables and cook for 10 minutes over low heat, stirring occasionally. Serve with roasted potatoes.

Yields 4 servings

STUFFED VEGETABLES
(MAHASHEE)

When I asked my grandmother why she undertook such a time-consuming task as stuffing vegetables—Why spend hours on a dish only to have it disappear within minutes?—her response was that stuffed vegetables were more interesting and more filling. Stuffed vegetables took her a long time to prepare because of the size of her family. "Stuffing vegetables just for you and your husband would take me no more time than a sneeze," she sniffed at me.

If the stuffing contains meat, then *mahashee* is considered a main course, and if not, it is considered a side dish, which Christian Arabs call *mahashee sayami*, or food for fasting.

BASIC RICE STUFFING
(HASHWEH)

1 cup uncooked rice
4 oz extra-lean ground beef
2 cloves garlic, *mashed*
1 tsp cumin
1 tbl allspice
1 tsp nutmeg
1 tsp saffron, *optional*
½ tsp black pepper

1. Wash and soak the rice in warm water for 1 hour. Put the drained rice in a bowl. Add the meat and spices to the rice and mix well.

Yields 1 cup

STUFFED ZUCCHINI
(KOOSA MEHSHEE)

Note: For variety, you can use the same coring and cooking method with Italian eggplants and green bell peppers.

8 zucchini,
no more than 6" in length
I cup Basic Rice Stuffing,
(see page 141)
6 cups water
½ cup tomato paste
4 cloves garlic, *mashed*
I tsp dried mint
pepper to taste

I. Core zucchini, leaving ¼-inch walls. Rinse in cold water and drain.

2. Using the rice stuffing, fill the zucchini about three-quarters full or within an inch of the end to allow for rice expansion.

3. Mix the water with the tomato paste, garlic, dried mint and pepper. Bring the water mixture to boil to make a thick tomato sauce. Drop the stuffed zucchini in the boiling tomato sauce and cook for 30 minutes over medium heat. Gently move the zucchini to a serving platter and the liquid into a soup dish.

Nutrient value per serving:

Calories	225
Fat	6 grams
Cholesterol	20 milligrams
Fiber	6 grams
Sodium	120 milligrams

Yields 4 servings

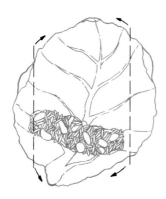  

How to Stuff Cabbage Leaves
(recipe on adjacent page)

STUFFED CABBAGE
(MEHSHEE MALFOOF)

3-lb head of cabbage
1 Basic Rice Stuffing,
(see page 141)
8 cloves garlic, *mashed*
½ cup lemon juice
1 tbl dry mint
water to cover cabbage
pepper to taste

Nutrient value per serving:

Calories	115
Fat	3 grams
Cholesterol	15 milligrams
Fiber	4 grams
Sodium	45 milligrams

1. Core the cabbage, and then blanch the head in boiling water for about a minute. The result will be that you can separate the outer cabbage leaves easily from the head. Repeat this process until the entire head has been peeled.

2. Slice the big leaves in half by removing the ribs. Save them. There is no need to cut the ribs out of the smaller leaves. In the pan, place a tablespoon of stuffing on each leaf. (See illustration.) Spread lengthwise and roll. Place a layer of the cabbage ribs cut from the large leaves. This will protect the rolls from any burning that might occur. Then arrange the rolls in compact rows over a layer of cabbage ribs. Gently squeeze each roll when placing in the pan. Sprinkle a little of the mashed garlic between each layer. Pour in enough water to cover the rolls by 2-inches. Place a light weight, such as a flat dish, over the cabbage so the rolls will remain firm and intact. Cook over medium heat for 35 minutes.

3. Mix the rest of the garlic, the lemon juice and the mint. Pour this mixture over the stuffed cabbage and cook over low heat for another 10 minutes.

Yields 8 servings

STUFFED GRAPE LEAVES
(MAHSHEE WARAQ ENAB)

100 grape leaves,
fresh or canned
1 cup Basic Rice Stuffing,
(see page 141)
10 cloves garlic
¼ cup lemon juice
pepper to taste

Nutrient value per serving:

Calories	100
Fat	3 grams
Cholesterol	15 milligrams
Fiber	1 gram
Sodium	15 milligrams

1. Blanch the grape leaves in hot water for a few seconds. Place a full teaspoon of the rice stuffing on the edge of the dull side of the leaf. Roll the leaf once, then fold in the sides and continue rolling. (See page 40.) The stuffed grape leaves should be the same size. Some of them may require more folding of the sides than others to achieve this uniformity. My mother insists they are more presentable this way, but the taste is the same.

2. Place a few unstuffed grape leaves in the bottom of the pot to avoid burning the bottom layer of rolls. Arrange the rolls in compact rows. Place the garlic between the layers. Add water to cover the rolls by 1-inch.

3. Place a china dish or a lid of a smaller pan on top of the rolls so they will remain firm and intact. Cook over medium heat for 35 minutes. Add the lemon juice, lower the heat and cook for an additional 10 minutes.

4. To unmold, choose a plate with a diameter at least 2-inches wider than the diameter of the cooking pan. Place it over the pot and invert it. Wait 10 minutes then remove the pot. You will have a cake shaped mold of stuffed grape leaves. This dish is usually served with yogurt.

Yields 6 servings

STUFFED POTATOES
(MEHSHEE BATATA)

8 medium potatoes
1 cup chopped onion
1 tbl olive oil
8 oz extra-lean ground beef
1 tbl allspice
½ cup tomato paste
4-5 cups water
pepper to taste

Nutrient value per serving:

Calories	370
Fat	9 grams
Cholesterol	20 milligrams
Fiber	6.5 grams
Sodium	120 milligrams

1. Peel the potatoes, then hollow a pocket in them, leaving ½-inch walls, which you should try not to pierce. To prevent a change of color, place the potatoes in cold water until you're ready to use them. Sauté the onions. Add the meat and allspice then cook for 5 minutes. Stuff the potatoes and arrange them upright in a pan. Mix the tomato paste and water and season black pepper. Pour the tomato sauce over the potatoes and cook over medium heat for 30 minutes.

Yields 4 servings

MID-EASTERN TORTELLINI IN YOGURT SOUP
(SHOUSHBARAK)

1 medium onion,
finely chopped
1 tbl oil
4 oz extra-lean ground beef
1 tsp allspice
4 cloves garlic, *mashed*
1 cup chopped cilantro
2 loaves Bread dough,
(see page 28)
3 pints Yogurt Soup,
(see page 99)
pepper to taste

Nutrient value per serving:

Calories	240
Fat	4.5 grams
Cholesterol	15 milligrams
Fiber	1.5 grams
Sodium	160 milligrams

1. Sauté the onions in the oil until transparent. Add the meat and allspice. Cook until it is done. Mix garlic and the cilantro together, then add about half of it to the meat. Cook for 2–3 minutes.

2. Roll the dough ⅛-inch thick and cut into 2-inch rounds. Place a teaspoon of filling in center of each circle. Fold the circle in half and pinch the edges together, as below. Place these tortellini on a cookie sheet and bake at 350° for 5 minutes.

3. Bring the Yogurt Soup to a boil. Add the water, pepper and the rest of the garlic-cilantro mix. Return to the boiling point, and then lower the heat. Carefully add the tortellini (*shoushbarak*) to the yogurt. Cook for 20 minutes, stirring as often as needed to prevent sticking.

Yields 8 servings

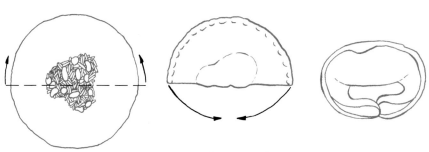

How to Make Tortellini

CHICKEN IN TOMATO SAUCE
(SHESH TAWOOK)

1 hot chili pepper
1 lb chicken breast
16-oz can of diced tomatoes
2 cloves garlic, *mashed*
½ cup lemon juice
1 tbl tomato paste
pepper to taste

Nutrient value per serving:

Calories	180
Fat	3 grams
Cholesterol	70 milligrams
Fiber	1.5 grams
Sodium	90 milligrams

1. Cut the chicken breast into 2-inch cubes. Cut the hot chili pepper into 2 halves and mix with the tomatoes, garlic, lemon juice, and pepper. Marinate the chicken in this tomato sauce at for least 2 hours, but overnight is better.

2. Discard the hot pepper and place the chicken and sauce in a baking dish. Cover with foil and bake at 375° for 30 minutes. Uncover and continue to bake for another 10 minutes or until the chicken is done.

Yields 4 servings

CHICKEN AND PITA BREAD IN CUMIN-YOGURT SAUCE
(FATET DJAJ)

1 lb skinned chicken breast
2 loaves pita bread
1 qt Cumin-Yogurt sauce,
(see page 78)
2 tbs pine nuts
¼ cup chopped parsley
pepper to taste

Nutrient value per serving:

Calories	370
Fat	7.5 grams
Cholesterol	75 milligrams
Fiber	5 grams
Sodium	375 milligrams

1. Simmer the chicken for about 20 minutes or until it is done. Cut the chicken into small pieces about ½-inch thick. Return the chicken to the stock.

2. Cut the bread into 1-inch squares. Place them in a baking dish and bake at 350° for 10 minutes until crisp and golden.

3. Just before serving, put the chicken on top of the bread, then pour on some of the hot chicken stock to cover the bread. Pour the Cumin-Yogurt Sauce on top, making sure it covers the entire pan. Roast the pine nuts in a 300° oven until golden. Then spread them and the parsley over the yogurt sauce.

Yields 4 servings

CHICKEN IN PITA BREAD WITH SUMAC
(MOUSAKHAN)

1 lb skinned chicken breasts
3 cups onion, *sliced*
1 tbl olive oil
⅓ cup sumac
4 whole wheat pita breads

Nutrient value per serving:

Calories	350
Fat	8 grams
Cholesterol	70 milligrams
Fiber	7 grams
Sodium	375 milligrams

1. Cover the chicken in water and cook for about 20 minutes or until the breasts are done. Remove them from the water and cut them into 1-inch pieces.

2. Sauté the onion in the oil until transparent, then mix with the chicken and the sumac.

3. Cut each pita bread in half. Stuff each half with the chicken-onion mixture. Place the stuffed halves next to each other in an oiled baking pan, and spray with olive oil spray. Bake at 400° for 20 minutes.

Yields 4 servings

BARBECUED CHICKEN
(DJAJ MASHWEE)

In the Levant, people rarely barbecue at home, but when families go on a picnic, they often take charcoal and other necessities. Then, while the women prepare salads and other side dishes, the men barbecue, usually chicken but sometimes lamb kebabs. Near the sea, many outdoor restaurants specialize in barbecuing. Some restaurants will slaughter the chicken only after you have ordered it; at others the fish will be caught only when you have chosen a fish dish. Barbecued foods are served with pure garlic sauce. I have seen American relatives who have "pigged out" on pure garlic and chicken take to their beds for three or four days until they have recovered from the bouts of overeating inspired by this tasty treat.

1 lb chicken breasts
1 cup Garlic Lemon Sauce,
(see page 75)
1 tbl black pepper

1. In a large mixing bowl combine all the ingredients and marinate the chicken for a couple hours in the refrigerator, turning the chicken breasts over several times. Barbecue the chicken over charcoal until cooked.

Nutrient value per Serving:

Calories	220
Fat	9 grams
Cholesterol	280 milligrams
Fiber	0
Sodium	250 milligrams

Yields 4 servings

STUFFED EGGPLANT WITH CUMIN-YOGURT SAUCE
(FATET MAKDOUS)

2 large eggplants
2 cups chopped onions
1 tbl olive oil
4 oz extra-lean ground beef
1 tsp allspice
pepper to taste
2 cups water
½ cup tomato paste
½ tsp black pepper
1 clove garlic, *mashed*
2 loaves of whole-wheat pita bread
2 cups Cumin-Yogurt Sauce
(see page 78)

Nutrient value per serving:

Calories	270
Fat	6.5 grams
Cholesterol	15 milligrams
Fiber	7.5 grams
Sodium	250 milligrams

1. Cut the eggplants into ½-inch thick slices. Place them on a cookie sheet, spray with olive oil spray and broil on both sides until golden.

2. Sauté the onions in the oil. Add meat and seasoning and cook for 15 minutes. Mix water, tomato paste, black pepper and garlic, then bring it to a boil.

3. Cut the pita bread into approximately 1-inch squares. Place the squares on a cookie sheet and bake at 350° until the bread is crisp and golden.

4. In a serving dish, first lay out the toasted bread. Second, put the eggplant on top of the bread. Third, spread the meat mixture on top and pour just enough of the tomato sauce to barely cover the bread. Both the eggplant and the sauce should be hot. Last, pour the yogurt sauce on top, trying to cover the previous layers.

Yields 6 servings

CHICKEN IN HOT SAUCE
(DJAJ BEL HAR)

1 lb skinned chicken breast
1 tbl hot red pepper
1 tbl olive oil
4 medium onions, *sliced*
½ cup tomato paste
1 cup water

Nutrient value per serving:

Calories 290
Fat 7 grams
Cholesterol 70 milligrams
Fiber 5 grams
Sodium 150 milligrams

1. Cut the chicken into 2-inch pieces. Rub the chicken pieces with ½ teaspoon of red pepper, then sauté the chicken in the olive oil until golden. Remove from the pan, then put aside.

2. In the same pan, sauté the onions with a couple tablespoons of water until transparent. Return the chicken to the pan. Mix the tomato paste with the water and the rest of pepper. Pour on top of the chicken and the onions. Cook on medium heat for 10 minutes.

Yields 4 servings

THE MONTHLY MEETING

Istekbal *literally means "the welcome." Women and men did not socialize together; this resulted in the creation of the tradition of Istekbal. Each woman in the neighborhood would have a designated day in the month to have her female friends and relatives visit her. For example, my neighbor's day was the first Monday of each month. She would chase her husband to the coffee shop, and order the boys in the family to either go out to play, or stay in their rooms.*

BASIC SPICED BURGER
(KAFTA)

1 lb skinned chicken breast
1 large onion, *chopped*
1 cup parsley, *chopped*
½ red bell pepper
½ tsp black pepper
½ tsp allspice
¼ tsp nutmeg

1. Grind the meat in a food processor. Add the rest of the ingredients and grind them with the meat for a couple turns. Remove from the food processor, and adjust the seasoning to your taste. Mold into burger rounds and grill them.

Yields 4 burgers

Nutrient value per serving:

Calories	110
Fat	3 grams
Cholesterol	70 milligrams
Fiber	2.5 grams
Sodium	75 milligrams

(AL-ISTEKBAL)

Of course, tradition required that the hostess of the day have a wide variety of sweets available for the guests, and that daughters of marriageable age be invited with their mothers. The guests were served drinks made from pomegranate juice or rose water. There were active exchanges about the health of each women's family, and, of course, any other gossip of interest...

SPICED BURGER FINGERS IN TOMATO SAUCE
(KABAB HINDEE)

I Basic Spiced Burger recipe,
(see page 153)
2 medium onions, *sliced*
I tbl olive oil
I 16-oz can of diced
tomatoes
½ cup water
2 tbs tomato paste
pepper to taste

1. Mold the spiced burger into hot-dog shaped pieces about 2-inches long and 1-inch thick.

2. Sauté the onions in the oil until transparent. Add the diced tomatoes, water and tomato paste, and bring to a boil. Drop the burger fingers into this mixture and cook on medium heat for 20 minutes.

Yields 4 servings

Nutrient value per serving:

Calories	300
Fat	9 grams
Cholesterol	70 milligrams
Fiber	6 grams
Sodium	110 milligrams

After about an hour of this kind of visiting, when all the guests were sure to have arrived, the appetizers and desserts were served. When everyone had eaten, the tables and chairs were pushed aside and someone began playing the oud, a pear-shaped string instrument (which is actually the forerunner of the "lute," and, of course, the Spanish guitar), and someone else began beating the derbakki, a small hourglass-shaped clay drum. And the dancing began. It would go on for as long as four hours, and when it appeared that exhaustion was setting in, the hostess would serve coffee, the signal that the visit was over.

BAKED SPICED BURGER FINGERS
WITH VEGETABLES
(KAFTA)

I Basic Spiced Burger recipe,
(see page 153)
2 medium zucchini, *sliced*
2 medium potatoes, *sliced*
2 medium carrots, *sliced*
2 cups water
I cup tomato paste
½ tsp allspice
I clove

1. Mold the spiced burger meat into hot dog shapes, but about 2-inches long and 1-inch thick. Mix the vegetables. Place them in a baking dish. Put the burger fingers between them. Thoroughly mix the water, tomato paste, allspice and clove, then pour the mixture over the vegetables. Cover with foil and bake in a 375° oven for 50 minutes.

Yields 6 servings

Nutrient value per serving:

Calories	220
Fat	2 grams
Cholesterol	50 milligrams
Fiber	6 grams
Sodium	170 milligrams

In my aunt's home, our famous coffee grounds reader, Fatima, was called upon to read the grounds for the guests, who would all turn their cups upside down after finishing their coffee. Fatima would tell single women of marriageable age that somebody handsome was looking for them. The newlyweds were told that the next week would be a good one for them; and for me, because Fatima knew I had always dreamed of traveling to the United States, she would say that she saw a long trip in the coffee grounds. In either three days, three months, or three years, she couldn't be sure.

BAKED BURGER AND POTATO IN TOMATO SAUCE
(KAFTA WA BATATA)

2 medium potatoes
1 Basic Spiced Burger recipe,
(see page 153)
1 15-oz can of diced
tomatos
1 cup water
pepper to taste

Nutrient value per serving:

Calories	420
Fat	6 grams
Cholesterol	70 milligrams
Fiber	12 grams
Sodium	195 milligrams

1. Boil the potatoes for 5 minutes. Peel them and slice into ½-inch thick slices. Place the slices in a greased 12-inch round baking pan.

2. Mold the burger meat into hotdog shapes, about 2-inches long and 1-inch thick. Put these between and on top of the potatoes. Mix the tomatoes, water and pepper, and pour the sauce over the potatoes and burgers. Bake at 375° for 45 minutes, or until the meat is cooked.

Yields 4 servings

BAKED EGGPLANT
(MNAZALET ASWAD)

2 large eggplants
2 cups chopped onion
pepper to taste
1 tbl allspice
1 tsp nutmeg
1 tbl olive oil
8 oz extra-lean ground beef
1 15-oz can of diced tomato
1 tbl tomato paste

Nutrient values per serving:

Calories	215
Fat	9 grams
Cholesterol	70 milligrams
Fiber	8.5 grams
Sodium	60 milligram

1. Peel, then slice the eggplant into ½-inch thick slices. Put them on a cookie sheet, spray with olive oil spray and broil until golden brown.

2. Sauté the onions with the allspice and nutmeg in oil. Add the meat and continue sautéing until the meat is cooked (about 10 minutes over medium-low heat).

3. Arrange eggplant slices next to each other in a baking dish. Spread the meat mixture over the eggplant. Mix diced tomatoes with tomato paste, then pour over the eggplant slices. You may add water if the sauce is not sufficient to cover the eggplant. Bake at 375° for 35 minutes.

Yields 4 servings

STUFFED ARTICHOKE
(ARDISHOKE BEL LAHM)

8 artichoke bottoms
(or whole artichokes)
1 cup chopped onions
1 tbl olive oil
8 oz extra-lean ground beef
1 tbl allspice
pepper to taste
1 tsp nutmeg
1 cup water
1 clove garlic, *mashed*
1 tbl flour
3 tbs lemon juice
½ tsp white pepper

Nutrient value per serving:

Calories 245
Fat 9 grams
Cholesterol 70 milligrams
Fiber 14 grams
Sodium 250 milligrams

1. If you are using the whole artichokes, boil them in water for about 30 minutes. Remove from water, take off the leaves, and scoop out the choke. If you are using frozen or canned bottoms, just boil them for 10 minutes. Place the artichoke bottoms in a greased baking dish.

2. Sauté the onions in olive oil for a couple of minutes. Add the meat, allspice, pepper and nutmeg. Continue to cook over medium heat for 10 minutes. Set aside.

3. Mix water and garlic; heat to boiling. Remove from the heat and whisk in the flour, lemon juice and white pepper. Return to heat and cook until it thickens.

4. Scoop two tablespoons of the meat mixture on top of each of the artichoke hearts. Pour the lemon-flour sauce on top. Cover with foil and bake at 375° for 30 minutes.

Yields 4 servings

UPSIDE-DOWN RICE EGGPLANT MOLD
(MAKLOBEH)

1 lb boneless chicken breast
2 large eggplants
1 cup rice
3 cardamom seeds
1 tsp allspice
½ tsp black pepper

Nutrient value per serving:

Calories	380
Fat	4 grams
Cholesterol	70 milligrams
Fiber	5 grams
Sodium	80 milligrams

1. In a cooking pot bring 3 cups of water to a boil. Place the chicken in the boiling water and add the cardamom. Simmer for about 20 minutes or until the chicken is done. Remove from the water. Save 2½ cups of the chicken stock for cooking the rice.

2. Remove the skin from the eggplants and cut them into ½-inch slices. Place them on a cookie sheet, spray with olive oil spray and broil them until golden brown on both sides. (The traditional recipe calls for frying the eggplant, but they literally drink the oil in which they're fried, which adds calories and fat that you may not want.)

3. Place the chicken in the bottom of a cooking pot. Arrange the broiled eggplants on top of the chicken. Now put the rice on top of the eggplants. Pour the saved chicken stock into the pot and add allspice and black pepper. Cover and cook on low heat for 30 minutes, or until the rice is done.

4. Just before serving, turn the pot upside down on a plate. To do so, use a flat serving plate that is at least 2 inches wider than the cooking pot. Place the plate upside down on top of the pot, then, holding the serving plate with one hand, and with the other hand under the pot, turn the pot upside down as fast as you can manage it. (Usually I ask my husband to do it.) Leave the pot on top of the plate for 5 minutes; then after it's removed, you will have a nice mold.

Yields 4 servings

SWEET PEAS WITH CHICKEN
(BAZELLAH BEL DJAJ)

8 oz skinned chicken breast, *coarsely ground*

1 tbl olive oil

pepper to taste

2 cloves of garlic, *mashed*

1 cup chopped cilantro

4 cups water

1 cup tomato paste

1 lb tender sweet peas, *fresh or frozen*

2 carrots, *cut into ½-inch cubes*

1. Over low heat, sauté the meat in the olive oil. Add pepper, mashed garlic and the chopped cilantro and sauté for 2–3 minutes. Add the water and the tomato sauce and bring it to a boil. Add the peas and the carrots and cook them over medium heat for 20 minutes.

Yields 4 servings

Nutrient value per serving:

Calories	330
Fat	7 grams
Cholesterol	70 milligrams
Fiber	9 grams
Sodium	240 milligrams

BAKED CHICKEN IN GARLIC LEMON SAUCE
(DJAJ BEL FERN)

2 potatoes
1 tbl olive oil
8 garlic cloves, *mashed*
½ cup lemon juice
1 cup water
1 tsp paprika
1 tsp thyme
2 skinned chicken breasts

Nutrient value per serving:

Calories	250
Fat	7 grams
Cholesterol	75 milligrams
Fiber	1.5 grams
Sodium	70 milligrams

1. Boil the potatoes for 10 minutes. Remove from water and slice into ½-inch thick slices.

2. Mix the olive oil, the garlic, the lemon juice, water, paprika and thyme. Cut the chicken breasts into 4 pieces. Dip the pieces in the olive-garlic mix, and place them in a baking dish. Fit the potatoes between the chicken. Pour what is left of the oil mixture on top of the chicken. Cover the baking dish with foil and bake at 375° for 30 minutes. Then uncover and bake for another 15 minutes or until the edge of the potatoes turn golden brown.

Yields 4 servings

CHICKEN WITH BULGUR AND CHICKPEAS
(BURGHUL MA'A HUMMUS WI DJAJ)

1 lb skinned chicken breast
5 cups water
1 cup #3 bulgur wheat
1 cup cooked chickpeas
pepper to taste

Nutrient value per serving:

Calories	385
Fat	5 grams
Cholesterol	70 milligrams
Fiber	10 grams
Sodium	80 milligrams

1. Simmer the chicken in water until done, then remove from the pan and let it cool. Save 2½ cups of the chicken stock. Cut the meat into small pieces, and return it to the stock. Bring to a boil, add the bulgur, the chickpeas, and the pepper and cook over medium heat for 45 minutes or until the bulgur is no longer chewy and the water has evaporated.

Yields 6 servings

وجعلنا من الماء كل شيء حي

"And we made every living thing from water."

BARBECUED FISH
(SAMAK MISHWEE)

2 lbs white fish
1 tbl olive oil
¼ cup lemon juice
1 tsp black pepper
½ tsp cumin
½ tsp paprika
½ tsp anise seed
2 cloves garlic, *mashed*

Nutrient value per serving:

Calories	165
Fat	4 grams
Cholesterol	75 milligrams
Fiber	0
Sodium	125 milligrams

1. Wash and clean the fish. Combine all the other ingredients in a bowl and marinate the fish in this mixture for a couple hours in the refrigerator. Close tightly—otherwise everything in the refrigerator will smell of fish.

2. Barbecue the fish over charcoal for 10 minutes or until it easily flakes. You can also bake the fish at 400° for 20 to 30 minutes or until it flakes. To prevent the fish from drying, wrap it in aluminum foil.

Yields 6 servings

BAKED FISH IN TAHINI SAUCE
(SAMAK BEL TAHINI)

2 lbs white fish
½ tsp black pepper
1 tbl olive oil
1 cup Basic Tahini Sauce,
(see page 76)
¼ cup lemon juice
2 cloves garlic, *mashed*
2 large onions, *sliced*

1. Wash the fish and dry. Sprinkle with pepper and brush with olive oil. Place the fish in a baking pan and bake in 400° oven for 20 minutes.

2. Mix the Basic Tahini Sauce with lemon and garlic. Take the fish from the oven, cover with the sliced onions and tahini-lemon sauce. Return to the oven for 10-15 minutes or until fish flakes easily with a fork.

Yields 6 servings

Nutrient value per serving:

Calories	260
Fat	8 grams
Cholesterol	75 milligrams
Fiber	2.5 grams
Sodium	135 milligrams

"A pot has found its lid."

CANNED TUNA WITH SPICY RED SAUCE
(TOON HAR)

This is a very tasty alternative to tuna salad.

2 cloves garlic, *mashed*
1 tbl olive oil
1 small onion,
finely chopped
1 red bell pepper,
finely chopped
¼ cup lemon juice
½ tsp ground coriander
½ tsp ground red pepper
1 12-oz can water-packed tuna

1. Sauté the garlic in olive oil for one minute. Add the onion, chopped red pepper and continue to sauté for 5 minutes. Remove from the heat. Add lemon juice, coriander and ground red pepper.

2. Mix sauce with the tuna and serve.

Yields 3 servings

Nutrient value per serving:

Calories	210
Fat	5 grams
Cholesterol	20 milligram
Fiber	1 gram
Sodium	80 milligrams

SEA BASS WITH SPICY WALNUT SAUCE
(SAMKEH HARA)

2 lbs sea bass or other similar fish
½ tsp black pepper
1 tbl olive oil
1 cup Spicy Walnut Sauce, (see page 79)
½ cup water
¼ cup lemon juice
1 tbl tomato paste

1. Clean the fish, then rub with the pepper and the olive oil. Bake the fish uncovered in an oiled pan at 400° for about 15 minutes. Remove the fish from the oven.

2. Mix the walnut sauce, water, lemon juice and tomato paste. Spread this sauce on top and inside the fish. Return it to the oven and bake for another 10 minutes, or until the fish is flaky.

Yields 6 servings

Nutrient value per serving:

Calories	210
Fat	8 grams
Cholesterol	65 milligrams
Fiber	1 gram
Sodium	120 milligrams

FISH WITH TAHINI
AND PARSLEY SAUCE
(SAMAK BEL-TARATOUR)

¼ cup lemon juice

2 cloves garlic, mashed

½ tsp black pepper

2 lbs fish of your choice, preferably sea bass or halibut

2 cups Tahini and Parsley Sauce, (see page 77)

1. Mix lemon juice, garlic and black pepper. Rub the fish inside and out with this liquid. Bake uncovered in an oiled pan at 400° for about 20–30 minutes until the fish is flaky.

2. Pour the Tahini and Parsley Sauce over the fish and serve.

Yields 6 servings

Nutrient value per serving:

Calories	200
Fat	6 grams
Cholesterol	65 milligrams
Fiber	less then one gram
Sodium	110 milligrams

Chapter Eleven
Desserts

In Syria, on special occasions such as the celebration of the Eid (the Islamic holiday that celebrates the breaking of the Ramadan fast) and Christmas, it is customary to have a dessert table set in the family room all day long. Guests who do not help themselves to dessert, are usually served by the hostess. Actually, she will force-feed them with a sampling of every dessert she has prepared. I have seen hostesses vehemently insist on the guest eating, and after she has done all the feeding that propriety allows, her husband takes over and continues pushing food on the company. In many Levantine households, this routine—some call it the Levantine food torture—continues until every adult member of the family has had an opportunity to show their hospitality—at the expense of the guests, of course. Each family tries to out do its neighbors with the varieties of desserts offered. This family effort was apparently the genesis of many a professional pastry shop in Syria and Lebanon, as ownership of pastry shops remains in the family forever, never being sold to outsiders.

Unless one lives near the famous Arabic dessert bakeries here in the United States, or in London, Paris or Montréal, buying desserts is a problem. The pastry shops known to me are Shatila, in Dearborn, Michigan, which does a terrific mail-order business, the Mediterranean Bakery in Alexandria, Virginia, just outside of Washington, D.C., and Samadi, also in suburban Washington, D.C. Montréal is home to North America's largest Arabic supermarket and bakery. At Marché Adonis you can find every Arabic sweet or dessert imaginable and it is well worth a special visit if you are in the area. Living in South Dakota, I have to make celebration desserts at home. But I've created some wonderful shortcuts, and I've tried to make the desserts as healthy as possible and still call them desserts. My favorites—those I can prepare as low-calorie and low-fat treats and still make them tasty—are in this chapter.

SUGAR SYRUP
(QATER)

This syrup is used to sweeten most Levantine desserts.

3 cups sugar
3 cups water
2 tbls lemon juice
1 tbl orange blossom water
(*mai zahr*)

1. Dissolve the sugar in the water and boil rapidly. Remove the foam that rises to the top. Add lemon juice and continue boiling until the syrup resembles thin honey. To preserve the essence of the orange blossom water, add it just at the moment you turn off the heat.

Nutrient value per cup:

Calories	600
Fat	0
Cholesterol	0
Fiber	0
Sodium	10 milligrams

Yields 4 cups

COFFEE

Coffee is always served in homes with a glass of flavored water, such as orange blossom water, added to the coffee water. The hostess will also fill a dish on the serving tray with jasmine blossoms in order to buttress the aroma of the coffee.

The tradition is to offer sweets or fresh fruit to a guest, but the hospitality is not complete until coffee is offered. Because of the tradition of extraordinary hospitality, serving coffee becomes a polite way to signal that the visit is coming to an end.

MILK AND ORANGE PUDDING
(BALOUZA)

Milk pudding:

4 tbs cornstarch
½ cup water
4 cups skim milk
½ cup sugar
1 tbl orange blossom water

Orange topping:

2 cups orange juice
¼ cup sugar
¼ cup water
2 tbs cornstarch
1 tsp orange blossom water

Garnish, *optional*:

1 cup unsalted chopped pistachio nuts

Nutrient value per serving (without the pistachios):

Calories	335
Fat	1 gram
Cholesterol	4 milligram
Fiber	less then one gram
Sodium	145 milligrams

1. For the milk pudding, dissolve the cornstarch in the water. Heat the milk in a heavy pot over medium heat. Add the sugar and cornstarch mixture. Continue to simmer, stirring constantly with a wooden spoon. Be careful not to scrape the bottom of the pan. The milk may burn slightly at the bottom and if it is scraped it will give a burned taste to the whole pudding. When you feel a slight resistance while stirring, and the mixture coats the back of the spoon, it has thickened sufficiently. Add orange blossom water, stir and cook for 1 more minute. Remove the pan from the heat. Allow to cool slightly, then pour the pudding into ice cream dishes. Leave at least a ½-inch space at the top to make room for the orange topping. Let it cool while you are making the topping.

2. For the orange topping, follow the same steps as milk pudding, replacing the milk with orange juice. After you remove the topping from the heat, allow it to cool slightly. Pour approximately a ½-inch layer of the orange topping slowly on the milk pudding.

3. Chill and serve decorated with a pattern of chopped pistachios.

Yields 4 servings

PANCAKES STUFFED WITH RICOTTA
(KATAYEF BEL JEBNEH)

Pancakes, basic recipe:

1 cup skim milk

1 cup water

¾ cup flour

3 tbs cream of wheat

2 tsp baking powder

Stuffing:

1½ cup fat free ricotta cheese

Syrup:

¾ cup-1½ cups Sugar Syrup,

(see page 171)

Nutrient value per pancake:

Calories   75

Fat   less then one gram

Cholesterol   0

Fiber   less then one gram

Sodium   30 milligram

1. For the pancakes, mix all the pancake ingredients, cover and wait 10 minutes.

Pour a 3-inch pancake on to a hot griddle or skillet, and cook until the top of the pancake is bubbly and the edges become dry. Remove the pancake from the skillet. *It's important not to turn it over.* Put the pancakes on a towel and let them cool for 10 minutes. Make 20 pancakes in this way.

2. Place one 1 tbl of the cheese on top of each pancake. Fold over in half, and press the edges closed. Arrange the stuffed pancakes on a greased cookie sheet. Bake in a 350° oven for 10 minutes. Remove them from the oven and pour syrup on top of each one.

Yields 20 pancakes

PANCAKES STUFFED WITH WALNUTS
(KATAYEF BEL JOZ)

Pancakes:

I Basic Recipe,
(see page 173)

Stuffing:

I cup walnuts, *ground*
¼ cup sugar
I tbl orange blossom water
I tsp ground cardamom

Dressing:

¾ cup-1½ cups Sugar Syrup,
(see page 171)

Nutrient value per pancake:

Calories	145
Fat	4 grams
Cholesterol	0
Fiber	0.5 gram
Sodium	12 milligram

I. Pancakes: Follow the same steps in the previous recipe.

2. Stuffing: Mix all the stuffing ingredients. Place one teaspoon of the stuffing on top of each pancake. Fold in half and press the edges closed. Arrange in a greased baking pan and bake in a 350° oven for 10 minutes. Remove them from the oven and pour syrup on top of each one and serve.

Yields 20 pancakes

CHEESE PUDDING
(HALAWET AL-JEBEN)

1 cup water
1 cup Sugar Syrup,
(see page 171)
4 cups fat-free shredded
mozzarella cheese
1 cup cream of wheat

Nutrient value per serving:

Calories 355
Fat less then one gram
Cholesterol 13 milligrams
Fiber 1.5 grams
Sodium 640 milligrams

1. Mix the water and Sugar Syrup in a heavy pot and bring to a boil over medium heat. Turn the heat to medium low. Add cheese to the boiling syrup a ½-cup at a time, stirring constantly. When you finish adding the cheese, add the cream of wheat and continue stirring. The mixture will develop a dough-like texture. When the cream of wheat is all mixed in, remove from the heat and pour into a flat dish. Chill and serve.

Yields 6 servings

There are four degrees of sweetness available for coffee. Murra, slightly bitter, is without sugar. Al reeha is with just a touch of sugar. Wasat means medium sweet, but not syrupy. Hilweh is the sweetest, with about one teaspoon of sugar for one espresso-size cup, which is, in fact, quite syrupy.

The coffee is cooked in a special pot called the rakweh. I have seen a hostess employ up to four coffee pots in order to accommodate her guests. The coffee is served in special, espresso-size cups, some of which have designs emblazoned on the sides, and others with no design at all. It is considered poor manners to drink water immediately following coffee—the hostess may suspect that you needed to wash the coffee taste from the mouth. If one is thirsty, it is much more polite to drink water before coffee is served.

MILK AND RICE PUDDING
(RUZ BEL HALEEB)

5 cups skim milk
½ cup sugar
½ cup medium grain rice
1 tbl cornstarch
1 tbl orange blossom water

Nutrient value per serving:

Calories	195
Fat	less then one gram
Cholesterol	4 milligrams
Fiber	less then one gram
Sodium	105 milligrams

1. Wash and soak the rice in water for a ½ hour. Mix cornstarch in a cup of the milk. Put the rest of the milk in a saucepan, and add the rice, sugar and cornstarch mix. Place the saucepan on medium heat and bring the mixture to a boil, stirring continuously. When you feel a slight resistance while stirring and the mixture coats the back of the spoon, add the orange blossom water, stir and turn off the heat.

2. Allow the pudding to cool slightly, then pour it directly into ice cream dishes. Chill for at least 2 hours before serving.

Yields 6 servings

RICE SQUARES
(MUHALLABIA)

3 cups skim milk

¾ cup cream of rice

¼ cup sugar

1 tsp ground Arabic gum
(*mistki*)

¼ cup bread crumbs

1 tbl orange blossom water

Nutrient value per serving:

Calories	195
Fat	1 gram
Cholesterol	2 milligrams
Fiber	0.5 gram
Sodium	105 milligram

1. Place the milk in a heavy pan. Add the cream of rice and sugar, and stir continuously over medium heat for 10 minutes. Turn the heat to medium low, add the Arabic gum and continue stirring until the mixture thickens and begins to bubble. Remove the mixture from the heat and pour into a greased baking pan. Sprinkle the breadcrumbs evenly on top, and bake in a 400° oven until the breadcrumbs turn golden, about 10-15 minutes.

2. Remove from the oven and allow to cool slightly. Chill for an hour and cut into 2-inch squares just before serving.

Yields 6 servings

CREAM OF WHEAT SQUARES
(NAMMURA)

2 cups cream of wheat
1 cup nonfat plain yogurt
2 tbls canola oil
1 tsp baking powder
¾ cup Sugar Syrup,
(see page 171)
pine nuts or blanched
almonds, for decoration,
optional

Nutrient value per serving:

Calories 345
Fat 4 grams
Cholesterol 1 milligram
Fiber 2.2 grams
Sodium 25 milligrams

1. Mix all the ingredients except the syrup, pine nuts and almonds. Pour the mixture into a greased 9 x 12 x 3-inch pan. Shake the pan lightly in order to spread it evenly.

2. Bake at 350° for 15 minutes. Remove from the oven and cut the baked mixture into 2-inch squares. Place one pine nut or a whole almond on each square. Return to the oven and bake until golden brown, or about another 20 minutes. Pour the cold syrup over the hot squares until they are saturated. (Add more syrup if you like a sweeter taste.)

Yields 10 servings

إن كان حبيبك عسل ما تلحسوش كله

"Even if honey be your cup,
Restrain your taste: don't lick it all up."

Glossary

Arabic Gum: Made from special pine trees in the Middle East and used in making commercial gums and dessert. It is sold in Middle Eastern food stores.

Bulgur: Parboiled (boiled and dried) wheat. You can buy two types, white and red (which is actually light brown) bulgur; the difference comes from the kind of wheat that was boiled to make the bulgur. Bulgur is sold in bulk in health food stores and Middle Eastern food stores. It comes in three different sizes: #1, the finest, used in making *kibbeh*; #2, less coarse, used in salads such as *tabbouli*; #3, the most coarse, used for pilaf.

Harisa: A red hot pepper paste. Harisa is made by cutting hot red peppers, removing the seeds, placing the peppers on a flat surface, drying them in the shade for a couple of days, then pureeing them with salt and some olive oil.

Junket Rennet Tablets: An enzyme used to coagulate the protein in milk in order to make cheese.

Orange-Blossom Water: Diluted orange blossom extract. It is used widely in Eastern Mediterranean cooking because of its citrus flavor. If not available, vanilla extract can be used instead.

Pomegranate molasses: A concentrated syrup made from pomegranate juice, available in Middle Eastern food stores.

Pomegranate: A popular fruit in the Mediterranean. It has a round shape and tough skin; inside there are small rosy seeds pressed together. To remove the seeds, cut the pomegranate in half cross-wise. Place it in a dish, with the cut side down, and tap on top with a knife. The seeds will fall into the dish. Occasionally, in the right season, about October, you can find this fruit in supermarkets, but they are also available in Middle Eastern stores.

Tahini: A paste made from grinding sesame seeds. It is used to thicken and gives a distinctive nutty flavor to dishes like hummus and sauces like *tahini*.

Eggbeaters: The brand name of an egg substitute. It is made of egg whites with yellow coloring to give an egg-like color. If you cannot find it, use four egg whites in a recipe that call for two eggs.

Oil spray: Oil sprays, such as Pam, are used widely in the United States to cut down the fat in food. Pam is a mixture of oil and alcohol. You can replace it by whisking together water and oil and brushing the vegetables with the combination, making sure that you whisk continuously.

Where to Find Ingredients

Arizona
Haji Baba Middle Eastern Food
1513 East Apache
Tempe, AZ 85281
(480) 894-1905
(480) 966-4672

California
Al-Baraka Market
4135 Spulveda Boulevard
Culver City, CA 90230
(310) 397-6022

Al-Jibani Halal Market
23385 Golden Springs Drive
Diamond Bar, CA 91765
(909) 861-3865

Avocado Food Market
852 Avocado Avenue
El Cajon, CA 92020
(610) 588-1773

Fairuz Middle Eastern Grocery
9124 Foothill Boulevard
Cucamonga, CA
(909) 948-4312

Fresno Deli
2450 East Gettysburg Avenue
Fresno, CA 93726
(209) 225-7906

International Groceries
3548 Ashford Street
San Diego, CA 92111
(858) 569-0362

K & C Importing
2771 West Pico Boulevard
Los Angeles, CA 90006
(323) 737-2970

Levant International
9421 Alondra Boulevard
Bellflower, CA 90706
(562) 920-0623

Marhaba Supermarket
10932 East Emperial Highway
Norwalk, CA
(562) 868-2272

Middle East Food
26 Washington Street
Santa Clara, CA 95050

Near East Foods
4595 El Cajon Boulevard
San Diego, CA 92115
(619) 284-6361

P & J Deli Market
754 North Lake Avenue
Pasadena Lake Center
Pasadena, CA
(323) 887-8797

Samiramis Importing Company
2990 Mission Street
San Francisco, CA 94110
(415) 824-6555

Sweis International
6809 Hazeltine Avenue
Van Nuys, CA 91405
(818) 785-8193

Colorado
Middle East Market
2254 South Colorado Boulevard
Denver, CO 80222
(303) 756-4580

Connecticut
Nouzaim Middle Eastern Bakery
1650 East Main Street
Waterbury, CT 06705
(203) 756-0044

Florida
Ali Market
2901 West Oakland Park Boulevard
Fort Lauderdale, FL 33311
(954) 428-3739

Damascus Mid East Food
5721 Hollywood Boulevard
Hollywood, FL
(954) 962-4552

Illinois
Holy Land Grocery
4806-4808 North Kedzie Avenue
Chicago, IL 60625
(312) 588-3306

Middle Eastern Bakery
1512 West Foster Avenue
Chicago, IL 60640
(312) 561-2224

Maryland
Yekta Deli
1488 Rockville Pike
Rockville, MD 20800
(301) 984-1190

Massachusetts
Near East Baking Company
5268 Washington Street
West Roxbury, MA 02132
(617) 327-0217

Syrian Grocery
270 Shawmut Avenue
Boston, MA 02118
(617) 426-1458

Minnesota
Sinbad Café and Market
2528 Nicollet Avenue South
Minneapolis, MN 55404
(612) 871-6505

New Jersey
Al-Khayyam
7723 Bergenline Avenue
North Bergen, NJ 07047
(201) 869-9825

Fattal's Syrian Bakery
975 Main Street
Paterson, NJ 07503
(973) 742-7125

M & N Market, Inc.
28-01 Kennedy Boulevard
Jersey City, NJ 07306
(201) 963-8683

Nouri's Syrian Bakery
999 Main Street
Paterson, NJ 07503
(800) 356-6874

New York
El-Asmar International Delights
212 28th Street
Brooklyn, NY 11201
(718) 369-0820

Oriental Pastry and Grocery
170-172 Atlantic Avenue
Brooklyn, NY 11201
(718) 875-7687

The Family Store
69-05 3rd Avenue
Brooklyn, NY 11209
(718) 748-0207

North Carolina
Nur Deli
28 Hillsborough Street
Raleigh, NC 27606
(919) 832-6255

Ohio
Gus's Middle Eastern Bakery
308 East South Street
Akron, OH 44311
(330) 253-4505

Sinbad Food Imports
2620 North High Street
Columbus, OH 43202
(614) 263-2370

Oklahoma
Mediterranean Imports
36-27 North MacArthur
Oklahoma City, OK 73122
(405) 810-9494

Pennsylvania
Salim's Middle Eastern Food Store
47-05 Center Avenue
Pittsburgh, PA 15213
(412) 621-8110

Texas
Droubi's Bakery and Grocery
7333 Hillcroft
Houston, TX 77081
(713) 988-5897

Phoenicia Bakery and Deli
2912 South Lamar
Austin, TX 78704
(512) 447-4444

Worldwide Foods
2203 Greenville Avenue
Dallas, TX 75206
(214) 824-8860

Virginia
Halalco
108 East Fairfax Street
Falls Church, VA 22046
(703) 532-3202

Mediterranean Bakery
352 South Picket Street
Alexandria, VA 22304
(703) 751-1702

Canada
Abir Foods, Inc.
1272 A Eglinton Avenue East
Mississauga, Ontario
Canada L4W 1K8

Byblos Mini Mart
2667 Islington Avenue
Rexdale, Ontario
Canada M9V 2X6

Jerusalem Supermarket
3355 Hurontario Street #8
Mississauga, Ontario
Canada L5A 2H3

Nasr Foods
1996 Lawrence Avenue East
Scarborough, Ontario
Canada M1R 221

Marché Adonis
9590 de l'Acadie
Montréal, Quebec
Canada H4N 1L8

Supermarché Alchallal
475 Côte Vertu
Saint-Laurent, Quebec
Canada H4L 1X7

Provisions Byblos
175 Côte Vertu
Saint-Laurent, Quebec
Canada H4N 1C8

Marché Suidan
710 Boulevard Labelle
Chomedy, Laval, Quebec
Canada H7V 2T9

Mid East Food Centre
1010 Belfast Road
Ottawa, Ontario
Canada K1G 4A2

Lockwood Farm Market
699 Wilkins Street
London, Ontario
Canada N6C 5C8

Phoenicia Foods Ltd.
2594 Asgricola
Halifax, Nova Scotia
Canada B3K 4C6

Rosslyn Food Market
11316 134th Avenue
Edmonton, Alberta
Canada T5E 1K5

Elmasu Food Imports
3477 Commercial Street
Vancouver, British Columbia
Canada V5N 4E8

Index

Other Ethnic Cooking Titles of Interest

The Essential Olive Oil Companion
by Anne Dolamore • illustrated by Madeleine David
The healthy benefits of olive oil have been enjoyed for centuries throughout the Mediterranean but only recently are they being appreciated worldwide. This fascinating and unique book, both a history and a practical compendium, includes 100 traditional and regional olive oil recipes.

ISBN 1-56656-334-8 • $15.95 pb (in Canada, $22.95)
160 pages • full-color illustrations

A Taste of Lebanon
Cooking Today the Lebanese Way
by Mary Salloum
Covering all aspects of Lebanese cuisine—from appetizers and sauces to soups, salads, entrées, stews, stuffed vegetables, poultry, fish, meatless dishes, yogurt, savory pastries, pita bread fillings, and sweets—this book offers simple step-by-step instructions to guide the novice or experienced cook through more than 200 mouth-watering dishes.

ISBN 0-940793-90-3 • $15.95 pb (in Canada, $22.95)
190 pages • 17 full-color photos

A Taste of Latin America
Recipes and Stories
by Elisabeth Lambert Ortiz
"A beguiling blend of delicious recipes, engaging personal anecdote and fascinating historical background. A thrilling insight into the tastes, the life and the culture of Latin America."
—*Claudia Roden*

ISBN 1-56656-287-2 • $15.00 pb (in Canada, $20.00)
128 pages • b&w illustrations

Richard Olney's French Wine and Food
A Wine Lover's Cookbook
by Richard Olney
"A tour de force from a culinary genius. This is one of the most evocative collections of menus I have ever encountered. And no one else writes so eloquently about wine. In matters of the palate I always trust Richard Olney."
—*Paula Wolfert*

ISBN 1-56656-226-0 • $17.95 pb (in Canada, $24.95)
128 pages • full-color photos

We strongly urge you to support your local bookstore.
To order directly, call **1-800-238-LINK** or visit **www.interlinkbooks.com**

From the Lands of Figs and Olives

Over 300 delicious and unusual recipes from the
Middle East and North Africa

by Habeeb Salloum and James Peters

"A delicious magic carpet ride through the Middle East
and North Africa."

—*The Toronto Sun*

One of the most complete books on the cuisine ever published,
providing a wealth of exciting new recipes as well as some of the best
traditional ones, carefully tested and adapted for the Western kitchen.

ISBN 1-56656-160-4 · $17.95 pb (in Canada, $24.95)
288 pages · full-color photos and b&w illustrations

Food for the Vegetarian

Traditional Lebanese Recipes

by Aida Karaoglan

This tantalizing collection of vegetarian recipes—passed down
from mother to daughter, generation after generation—has been
carefully collected from rural villages of Lebanon, patiently
tested and adapted to Western kitchens.

ISBN 1-56656-105-1 · $15.95 pb (in Canada, $21.95)
165 pages · full-color photos

Caribbean and African Cooking

by Rosamund Grant   foreword by Maya Angelou

"When Rosamund Grant invites us to join her Caribbean
feasts we can almost hear reggae, sitar, and Spanish music…
I like this kind of writing and I like this kind of invitation."

—*Maya Angelou*

"Beautiful, concise and deeply ethnic."

—*The Observer (London)*

ISBN 1-56656-275-9 · $15.00 pb (in Canada, $21.00)
128 pages · full-color photos

A Taste of Madras

A South Indian Cookbook

by Rani Kingman

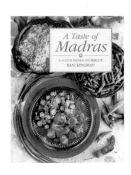

"Highly recommended: a must for cooks of Indian cuisine."

—*The Bookwatch*

"The food of southern India is a delight… this book is both
a good introduction for those wanting to get their tongues wet
and a nice addition to the cookbook library of those who've
already had the pleasure of digging into *masala dosais*."

—*The Asian Foodbookery*

ISBN 1-56656-195-5 · $17.95 pb (in Canada, $24.95)
160 pages · full-color photos